The Complete Guide to

PROJECT MANAGEMENT

for New Managers and Management Assistants

How to Get Things Done in Less Time

By Elle Bereaux

THE COMPLETE GUIDE TO PROJECT MANAGEMENT FOR NEW MANAGERS AND MANAGEMENT ASSISTANTS: HOW TO GET THINGS DONE IN LESS TIME

ISBN-13: 978-1-60138-010-4   ISBN-10: 1-60138-010-0

Library of Congress Cataloging-in-Publication Data

Bereaux, Elle, 1957-
  The complete guide to project management for new managers and management assistants : how to get things done in less time / by Elle Bereaux.
       p. cm.
  Includes bibliographical references.
  ISBN-13: 978-1-60138-010-4 (alk. paper)
  ISBN-10: 1-60138-010-0 (alk. paper)
  1. Project management. I. Title.
  HD69.P75B467 2008
  658.4'04--dc22
                         2007052810

COVER & INTERIOR LAYOUT DESIGN: Vickie Taylor • vtaylor@atlantic-pub.com
PROOFREADER: Cathy Bernardy • bernardyjones@gmail.com

·Printed in the United States

Printed on Recycled Paper

Author Dedication

*To my husband, David, for encouraging
me to reach.*

We recently lost our beloved pet "Bear," who was not only our best and dearest friend, but also the "Vice President of Sunshine" here at Atlantic Publishing. He did not receive a salary but worked tirelessly 24 hours a day to please his parents. Bear was a rescue dog that turned around and showered myself; my wife Sherri; his grandparents Jean, Bob and Nancy; and every person and animal he met (maybe not rabbits) with friendship and love. He made a lot of people smile every day.

We wanted you to know that a portion of the profits of this book will be donated to The Humane Society of the United States.

— *Douglas & Sherri Brown*

THE HUMANE SOCIETY
OF THE UNITED STATES©

The human-animal bond is as old as human history. We cherish our animal companions for their unconditional affection and acceptance. We feel a thrill when we glimpse wild creatures in their natural habitat or in our own backyard.

Unfortunately, the human-animal bond has at times been weakened. Humans have exploited some animal species to the point of extinction.

The Humane Society of the United States makes a difference in the lives of animals here at home and worldwide. The HSUS is dedicated to creating a world where our relationship with animals is guided by compassion. We seek a truly humane society in which animals are respected for their intrinsic value and where the human-animal bond is strong.

Want to help animals? We have plenty of suggestions. Adopt a pet from a local shelter, or join The Humane Society and be a part of our work to help companion animals and wildlife. You will be funding our educational, legislative, investigative, and outreach projects in the United States and across the globe.

Or perhaps you'd like to make a memorial donation in honor of a pet, friend, or relative? You can through our Kindred Spirits program. If you'd like to contribute in a more structured way, our Planned Giving Office has suggestions about estate planning, annuities, and even gifts of stock that avoid capital gains taxes.

Maybe you have land that you would like to preserve as a lasting habitat for wildlife. Our Wildlife Land Trust can help you. Perhaps the land you want to share is a backyard — that's enough. Our Urban Wildlife Sanctuary Program will show you how to create a habitat for your wild neighbors.

So you see, it's easy to help animals, and The HSUS is here to help.

The Humane Society of the United States
2100 L Street NW
Washington, DC 20037
202-452-1100
www.hsus.org

Acknowledgements

In compiling this work, I interviewed project managers all over the United States. Some of them had 20 years of experience; others were in their second year. I spoke with people in the private sector and in the government. I learned that some project managers use many types of highly sophisticated, specialized software while others find as much success employing simple spreadsheets.

I wish to thank every project manager for his or her time, the tips offered for this work, and the experiences they all shared. I would like to pay special acknowledgement to the people listed below. You will find the wisdom they share throughout this work.

Project Manager	Company	Experience
Bob Eckert	Deluxe (Business Products & Services)	24 Years
Mike Heutmaker	Digi International (Communications)	5 Years
Sary Mabjish	Withheld (Pharmaceutical)	4 Years
Christina Majeed	NexTec (Medical Software)	2 Years
Dan Mason	Withheld (Real Estate)	2 Years
Peggy Sanchez	Digi International (Communications)	1 Year
Paul Schoen	Bureau of Criminal Apprehension (Gov't)	13 Years
Karen Thomas	Withheld (Communications)	19 Years
Mike Tulipon	Withheld (Retail Buyer)	6 Years
Binh Vo	Withheld (Communications)	10 Years
Joseph Zubay	LinkIndigo (Consulting)	8 Years

Table of Contents

Author Dedication..3

Acknowledgements 6

Foreword...14

Introduction 17

Part 1: Determining the Project's Desired Results, Phases,& Life Cycle 21

Chapter 1: Management to Project Management 25

What Is a Manager Today? 25

Finding Your Own Managerial Style...........................34

What Is a Project Manager? 39

What Is a Project, Exactly? 39

What Is Project Management?...................................40

How Is Project Management Deployed?......................................40

Why Use Project Management?..41

Chapter 2: Preparing For Project Management 47

What are the Skills for Success? 51

Part 2: Identifying, Implementing, & Measuring Your Project's Actions 57

Chapter 3: Who Is Flying Your Plane? 59

How to Determine a Project's Phases...59

Five Generic Phases of Project Management............................60

Putting Processes and Phases Together......................................62

Chapter 4: Systems Check 67

Phase I: Demonstrate Project Need and Feasibility 71

Initiate Phase I 71

Plan Phase I..73

Execute Phase I 78

Building Your Team..78

The "Volunteered" Team Members...81

Put Benchmarks and Rewards in Place 82

Control and Close Phase I.. 82

Chapter 5: Choose a Runway 85

Phase II: Create the Project Plan (Part One) 87

Initiate Phase II 87

Describe the Project's Scope 88

Action 1: Create a Work Breakdown Structure 88

Action 2: Define the Project's Activities and
Succession (Activity List) 98

Action 4: Estimate the Duration of Each Activity.................... 105

Action 5: Assign Resources to Each Activity and Prepare
the Schedule.. 112

Action 6: Create the Project Schedule and its Associated
Gantt Chart 122

Action 7: Estimate the Costs 128

Chapter 6: Clearing for Takeoff 135

Phase II: Create the Project Plan (Part Two) 135

Action 8: Create Your Project's Budget 136

Action 9: Create a Variance Plan 138

Action 10: Establish the Quality Constraints........................... 140

Action 11: Create a Communications Plan............................142

Action 12: Create a Risk Management Plan 149

Action 13: Create the Project Plan...................................152

Close Phase II...152

Chapter 7: Takeoff 155

Phase III: Create a Draft of the Deliverables...........................155

Initiate Phase III..155

Plan Phase III..156

Meaningful Progress Meetings......................................156

Determine the Need for a Meeting..................................160

Effective Preparation 160

Begin on Time..162

Lead the Team to Participation.....................................162

Close the Meeting 163

Tips on Meetings from the Project Managers 163

Execute & Control Phase III 167

Progress Reports 169

Change Requests 173

Abandoning a Project..175

Chapter 8: Communicate With The Tower .. 179

Phase IV: Create the Deliverables 179

Controls 179

Initiate Phase IV 179

Plan Phase IV 180

Execute Phase IV 182

Effective Control Tools 182

Control Phase IV 183

Earned Value Management 184

Close Phase IV 187

Chapter 9: Happy Landings 189

Phase V: Test-Market & Release the Deliverables to Market 189

Initiate Phase V 189

Plan Phase V 189

Test-market the Deliverable 190

Execute and Control Phase V 193

Prepare for Final Deliverables 193

Prepare for Closure 193

Close Phase V 194

Terminating Your Project..194

Accept the Results of the Project 198

Part 3: Rocket Tools: Propel Your Project Management Skills to the Stratosphere......... 201

Chapter 10: Multiple Projects = Air Traffic Control 203

Assess the Scope of Deliverables 205

Assess Risks 212

Launch One Project Among Many 213

Manage People's Activities to Avoid Conflicts...........214

Prepare the Statement of Work...................................216

Prepare Work Breakdown Structure...........................217

Interact with Other Project Members.........................217

Report Progress 218

Change, Inevitable Change...219

Chapter 11: Software Is Not Rocket Science 223

Integrated Project Management Software 226

Software: Types 235

Effectively Using the Internet, Voice Mail, and Software 237

Voice Mail 237

E-mail. 238

Chapter 12: Aliens Among Us? 241

Conclusion 245

Appendix A: Top Reasons Project Managers Succeed or Fail 249

Appendix B: Project Studies 259

Glossary 265

References 279

About the Author 285

Index 287

Foreword

By Bob Eckert

Becoming a new project manager can be somewhat of a daunting task. It is always stressful to juggle various projects with many different personality types. Fortunately, *The Complete Guide to Project Management* addresses your concerns and will help you make a smooth transition into becoming a project manager.

Having been a project manager for 17 years, I have been hit with the toughest of tasks and the most difficult of people. Sometimes it was frustrating trying to figure out exactly what to do. I wish that I had a guide, such as this book, to help me when I first took on the job. It would have made things much more helpful and simplified the entire process.

The first thing you need to do when you become a project manager is learn exactly what you are doing and know what results you need. That is where this book begins. Elle Bereaux walks you through the process from beginning until the end. The only thing you will have to do is apply the steps to your particular project.

While the blueprint may be simple, handling the different people on your team may be difficult or uncomfortable. Fortunately, Bereaux gives you pointers for success on how you can handle the people on your team. The case studies that are scattered throughout the book provide invaluable tips and experiences so that you can see what other project managers have dealt with.

The project is not over when it ends. While this may seem contradictory, it is not. Once the project is complete, you need to assess the project and see what was successful and unsuccessful about the process. This assessment will help you realize what you can do in the future to become a better project manager. So many people forget this step in the process and move from project to project without learning. Bereaux addresses this issue and tells you what you need to know so that you can learn more about yourself and your own management style.

Realizing the strengths and weaknesses of your team will always help you prevail through tasks. Realizing your strengths and weaknesses will help take you, as Bereaux points it, "to the stratosphere."

Bob has over 24 years of IT experience including Operations, Management, Strategic Planning and Project Management. He is a 30 year employee of the Deluxe Corporation and currently managing several IT Infrastructure projects. Bob continues to be engaged in process improvement efforts especially Project Management processes.

Bob is a volunteer of the Project Management Institute - Minnesota Chapter and is currently serving as the Chapter President.

About Bob's Company:

Building on our legacy as one of the top check producers in the North America, Deluxe has evolved into a trusted and valued advisor to financial institutions and small businesses.

A Fortune 1000 company with more than 8,000 employees, Deluxe helps financial institutions and small businesses grow their businesses through a wide range of innovative products and services in fraud prevention, customer loyalty and brand building.

Introduction

If you are a new manager who needs to learn how to use project management, this book will help you.

There are many opinions regarding the definition of a manager. You will find countless books about managerial styles and types. In addition to universities that school people in management, there are management institutions that take one's spirituality and personality type into consideration when developing one's exact style.

Do not be intimidated by this. You will develop your managerial style over the course of your career, no matter what age you are as you enter management. The most important thing to recognize is that your role is not to order people around; your role is to work them toward becoming self-directed. Your boss will measure you on the performance of your direct reports. Therefore, everything you do needs to be with their best performance in mind — no matter what kind of style you develop as a manager.

For now, focus on establishing a good basis of respect between you and your direct reports. This will involve setting standards, building trust and confidence, providing performance feedback, demonstrating motivation, being a good listener, adapting to change, and providing constant communication. One of the best methods for accomplishing all these things is by managing a project.

Successful project management demands that you listen to your sponsor (client) and your stakeholders (the people who benefit from the outcome). You and your team will analyze and substantiate the need to create the product or service that the project will generate. You will plan every aspect of activity that needs to occur and set standards to ensure your plans are accurate. After you give feedback to your sponsor and make required adaptations to your plans, you will then execute the project. As it launches, you will implement control measures and provide feedback, again adapt if necessary, and keep your team motivated if things do not turn out exactly as you had planned. Finally, you will close the project and provide evaluations to your crew. Your boss will evaluate you based on the outcome; therefore, staying focused on your team's success is vital.

This book is for people who are new to management and project management. It is intended to help you succeed in both arenas by providing you with pitfalls to avoid, as well as tips for success. It will not only address how to use typical software systems and how to manage conflict, but it will also walk you through the life cycle of a project and describe how to manage multiple projects at once using project management software. The steps described herein are based upon the Project Management Body of Knowledge (PMBOK), which is produced by the Project Management Institute (PMI) in Philadelphia. PMI was founded in 1969 and has more than 240,000 members in 160 countries. It is one of the leading project management institutions in the world.

By learning this process, you will propel your managerial skill set to levels that some experienced managers do not possess. Many seasoned managers today have worked their entire lives without ever doing a project and learning the importance of careful planning, honest communication, and conscientious control.

Conversely, consider that you will need help from other people at times to find solutions for problems that are new to you but not to them. This book will show you how to ask for help from subject matter experts when necessary.

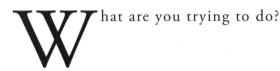

Part 1

Determining the Project's Desired Results, Phases, & Life Cycle

What are you trying to do?

You have a situation at work that needs a solution. The first question you need to answer is, what do you want to produce? What are you trying to do? The answer might seem obvious, but it deserves much thought, and you need to answer it fully to decide whether you even need a project or if the issue can be resolved with a simple action.

Examine your task and decide whether you need project management. First, identify what you want to produce. Second, decide who is required to accomplish the output. Third, identify whether what you are seeking is something that someone else is already doing or is accountable for doing. Next, get buy-in from your boss and, most important, from the sponsor who will provide the resources you require.

There are many things that employees do that are a part of their ordinary workday and do not require project management. Learn to distinguish these. Here are a few examples to compare and contrast:

- Writing a sales letter to a prospect versus publishing a sales manual for the division

- Managing the office's petty cash account versus planning an employee-awards event

- Going to a meeting versus creating a series of promotional presentations to launch a new product

After you decide you have a project, delve deeper into what you are undertaking. All projects have a life cycle composed of phases. There are standard phases for various industries, as identified by Project Management Institute (PMI) of Philadelphia. Here, we will use a generic set of five phases:

1. Demonstrate the project's need and feasibility.

2. Describe the project's scope.

3. Quantify terms for deliverables.

4. Create the deliverables.

5. Test and implement deliverables.

In Part 1, we will explore how your project's results — or deliverables — will create your phases and life cycle. We will walk you through the activities associated with each phase, such as how to evaluate the need for the project. We will provide essential definitions of project management and further explore and apply the management skills required to oversee a project.

By the end of Part 1, you will be able to apply the concepts of project management — and management itself — and see how they apply to an actual project.

In Part 2, we will simulate all phases of a project, allowing you to walk through it as though you were working it. By the end of Part 2, you will be ready to complete your own project.

In Part 3, we will give you the tools needed for advanced project management. We will explore the various types of software that will allow you to manage multiple projects at once. Imagine, for instance, that you work at a Hollywood studio and are responsible for the progress of six or seven films at once. How would you keep track of producers, filming dates, dailies, paychecks, contracts, press releases, scheduling promotional events, artwork, and editing for all these potential blockbusters without a control medium at your service? Either you can learn to be a whiz at note taking, or you can rely on any of several capable mediums available for project management.

This book is designed with new managers in mind. It will give you a high-quality, usable education about project management. By the time you are finished, you will be able to apply what you read toward managing your first project. Then, as your experience level progresses, you can seek out higher levels of education. There are worldwide institutions available for people to learn more about this skill. We also provide additional resources for you to consider in the References section of this book.

Chapter 1

Management to Project Management

What Is a Manager Today?

Management today includes duties such as staffing, recruiting, training, developing, and directing. It also requires the manager to keep abreast of vast technological changes and different work environments. Today, a manager may have direct reports who telecommute or who are located in a remote city. This manager needs to use technology to connect with such employees. Measurement tools and software are becoming increasingly important to today's manager for evaluating every employee's output evenly.

As a new manager, you will need to get to know your team members and always be thinking about developing each one toward his or her own potential. A big part of that process is to challenge them by delegating and establishing goals for them.

A good first step is to speak to each member one-on-one to "break the ice." Ask each one to define his or her role and responsibility. This helps you understand the team member's function and ensures that your understanding is the same as his or hers. Next, ask him or her to define the roles and responsibilities of each of the other team members. This exercise can be beneficial for several reasons. First, it lets you hear everyone's function several times (from various people) and thereby educates you about what everyone does. But even more important, it quickly identifies someone who does not know what another does. This will allow you to spot areas where you can build teamwork simply by having one person assist another. It also provides the added benefit of cross-training people in your team.

Note: Ensure there are no physical or policy restraints that would prohibit you from asking one employee to share in another's work.

Also during these initial conversations, be certain to express that you care about each person as well as the achievement of the goals of your organization. Express that you intend to delegate to help the team members advance their own skills. This conveys that you will be expecting them to show you what they can do. Encourage them to let you know when something is concerning them or preventing them from achieving their best. Keep these meetings brief — less than 15 minutes if possible. You want to set the example of being friendly but succinct.

Many managers — especially new ones — find delegation difficult. They fear it shows they are incapable or unwilling to do their own work, or worse, that they expect their direct reports to do their job for them.

Delegation produces many benefits. Employees learn new skills and become more involved in the team goals. The company now has cross-trained people who can help when you need an emergency stand-in. This frees you up to work toward your own effectiveness and development.

There are a few rules to delegation. Never delegate personnel items, such as salary treatment, feedback, or appraisals. Do not delegate with an uneven hand — if Leticia is able to work at high levels and Sharon is not, do not dole out more to Leticia just because she can handle it. Be aware of people who are not ready or are already too busy, and do not let your people delegate to you. This can happen when they claim they are overburdened or uncomfortable with the skills required for a given job. Use those instances as opportunities to train them or pull in another team member to assist them.

If you have an assistant, he or she should be able to do your complete job (except personnel items) within six to nine months. Of course, you would not want to unload your entire role at one time. Rather, step up his or her skill set in pieces. This will keep you from falling into the trap of thinking you can never move on or take a vacation. If no one knows how to do what you do, how will you ever get away? What about when it is time for you to advance? You do not want your boss to pass you over because you are indispensable to your current department.

Of course, you do run the risk of having your assistant (or a team member) achieve advancement before or instead of you. Do not let that get to you. It is a reflection of the individual's work and not of yours. Just move on and get busy delegating to your next assistant.

Feedback to all your employees is critical to their success and yours. Indeed, several states now have laws that require every employee in companies with 50 or more people to receive annual, formal appraisals. Even without this law, you should participate in this practice. Even better, establish quarterly goals for each person and review them as they go. Having an informal, quarterly review allows the employee the opportunity to correct items as needed or to give you feedback about why things are not progressing well. By the time he or she receives the annual review, there should be no surprises on it.

If an employee is not performing up to standards, you can try breaking down the goals into smaller segments. For instance, if someone has a goal of producing 40 widgets per month and is falling short, consider breaking it down into 10 widgets per week. Sometimes just reducing the quantity will work. Other times, you will find yourself facing the disciplinary process.

Many companies have their own inner standards about how to treat someone who is performing substandard. The critical rule here is to never discipline the person in public. These conversations should be behind a closed door; otherwise, you risk disaster. In the worse case, the employee might seek litigation against you for personal angst; in the best-case scenario, your message might not be immediately discarded before the employee sulks away.

CASE STUDY: KAREN THOMAS

Karen Thomas has been a project manager for 19 years in the communications industry. She was the most experienced of all the project managers we interviewed, with a wealth of triumphant projects on her résumé. However, consider that she still remembers something that happened to her in her very first year, as follows:

"I will never forget how I learned about how important it is to hold criticism to a private setting. I had been a very successful sales person for a number of years when I was promoted to project manager. The sales branch that I worked in was a total mess, the worst in the region, mostly due to the branch manager's lack of sales experience and big ego. Everyone in the branch hated her because she would make outrageous demands of the sales people, but she did not have a clue how to do it, herself. So, everyone quietly deferred to the operations manager instead of her. It was kind of like, "Big bad boss wants me to spend my afternoon signing 2,000 letters, personally, in blue ink when I could be selling during that time. And the operations manager will quietly say, 'Sign one and have the rest copied in color. Then go sell.' This is the kind of nonsense that went on.

"As a result of this, most of the sales people really liked the operations manager and when I was promoted, she became my immediate boss and I was thrilled. Except, I had a really hard time with project management in the first few months. I kept stumbling, and my projects were never on time. I did not know how to get a grip, but I kept thinking I was a manager now so I was supposed to figure it out, that to go to my boss would mean I was too stupid to do the job.

"Months went by, and I was growing more and more sullen. Then, my boss's birthday was coming up and my team and I threw her a pizza party. We were all sitting around the lunch table, I and my team of project workers, and her. The atmosphere in the office was tense; branch results were poor — everyone was

CASE STUDY: KAREN THOMAS

in trouble. I tried to make conversation about how things would pick up soon, to brighten the group, when my boss turned to me and in front of the whole group she said, 'Karen, you are part of the problem. You hang on to things way too long. You need to step up when you cannot handle things.'

"I do not remember how I got through the rest of the meal, but I do remember being incredibly humiliated. About two years later, I finally thought of a suitable response to her. I should have said, 'Well, why did you wait so long to tell me so?' but of course, it was too late by then.

"After that incident, we were never the same. I lost my respect for her entirely. I transferred to another branch three months later. By the way, I did really well in project management, after that. This was partly because I had conquered my learning curve and partly because I had the best boss that I ever had in my entire career, in that branch. I excelled, with his support. And he never gave me any kind of negative feedback in front of others.

"This story wouldn't be worth telling if I did not end it by saying that I realized, later, that my old boss was right. I did hold on to things too long, and this trait was keeping me from being successful. New project managers are going to need to ask questions and discuss where they are struggling. Their bosses will expect them to do this. I just wish she wouldn't have used the public setting to deliver the message."

If you have done everything correctly, by the time you meet with your employee, he or she should be expecting the meeting. Ask how you can help and listen carefully. Do not think you already know why his or her performance is failing. Maybe there is a personal reason that you could have no way of knowing about.

Note: Never ask about an employee's personal life. By law, this information can only be volunteered to you.

What the employee tells you will decide how you proceed, of course. If there is a training issue or something in the department that you can fix, do so. If not, seek all means possible to get assistance. For instance, if the person is struggling with something personal and has volunteered that to you, encourage him or her to contact your company's employee assistance program, if available. If not, be careful not to recommend any kind of treatment or recourse. Many companies have been sued because a well-meaning person offered a "great child care center" or "Doctor Wonderful" and something went wrong. Keep the issue at the center of your conversation and avoid offering any personal advice.

Whenever possible, use the available resources in your company for guidance with personnel issues. Your human resources manager might become one of your best friends at work. Of course, if you are struggling, seek out advice from your own boss. He or she may want you to take training specific to the kind of problem.

What we just explored applies to any manager who manages a team. But what if you do not manage a team? What if you are in charge of a process or something broader in your company?

In this instance, the only thing you can focus on is your own performance. However, it is important to dissect the various realms of your responsibility as a separate, measurable thing. In this instance, the processes that your company has put into place are now each a member of your "team."

As an example, consider the operations manager named Paulette who reports to a central region vice president of sales at a telecommunications company. She has no direct reports but is responsible for compensating all the salespeople and administering the human relations (HR) policies for their group. She is responsible for budget forecasting and expenditures reporting. She assists the vice president with monthly sales reporting to the regional president. She also oversees supplying people with laptops and arranges training for the union-based clerical people that directly report to various sales managers across several states.

Paulette has several processes she relies on:

- In her role of compensation manager, she relies on two different software systems that the company uses. These systems show bookings of sales for two different product groups. She is responsible for pulling. results from both systems once a month, tallying them, and paying people based on what the systems report.

- In her role as HR manager, she is responsible for filling vacant positions and advertising internal jobs in the company job software. She is the first contact for any manager who has a question or issue about how to proceed with personnel issues. She communicates with headquarters about such issues, as necessary, and provides information accordingly.

- For equipment, she relies on an information technology manager who provides her with laptops and cell phones for the sales people.

- She uses a separate budget system that shows what each sales group has spent, by individual, and she compares that to the loaded budgeted dollars for each line item.

- She calls on a training manager who helps her identify what is available for the union-based clerical force and how they can proceed with their own advancement, and she relates that information to their respective managers.

- She uses Microsoft® programs such as Excel, Word, and PowerPoint to prepare reports for her boss. These reports relay how the group is performing, where people are failing, and where they are excelling. At the end of each quarter, Paulette prepares a report for her boss's boss, explaining how things are going.

So, who (or what) are Paulette's team members?

1. The two software systems that provide sales results

2. The software system that allows her to recruit people

3. The headquarters people who give her input about how to deal with personnel issues

4. The information technologies people who provide her with hardware to be disseminated

5. The union that gives her guidance about how to appropriately train people

6. The software system that reports the spending of her group against the budgeted dollars

7. Microsoft® applications

Honestly, if Paulette is doing an excellent job, her boss will not care whether there are problems in her world. But if all the salespeople are complaining that they are not being paid fairly, he will look to her to explain. If she tells him that the two software systems that provide sales reports are incompatible and that everyone across the country is experiencing the same problem, she has just identified the root of the problem.

In this example, there is not a person who is not performing — it is a system. And this system is one of Paulette's "team members." It is keeping her from achieving the results she desires, and if this company were smart, it would be assigning a project manager to address this issue for all its employees.

Although she might not have the power to eliminate the non-performing system, she can at least pinpoint how a system is failing her. Just as if she had people reporting to her, she needs to document and track the progress of this part of her team.

On the other hand, if no one else is experiencing trouble with these systems, it would point to an issue with Paulette, and it would be an opportunity for her to improve herself.

Therefore, even if your team members are not people, you still have to manage each element independently. The two marked differences between people and systems are:

1. You cannot directly affect the performance of a company-approved system (you can only communicate its failure to headquarters).

2. You cannot delegate to a system.

In Paulette's example, she might consider asking her colleague sales managers whether she might delegate to their support staff, providing this request is within union guidelines. Doing so might be an excellent way for Paulette to off-load some of her burden. More important, she might enhance the development of a person who would make a good manager.

Managing today boils down to keeping your team's performance in constant focus. By setting attainable goals, offering frequent and honest feedback, delegating across your team, and communicating how your team's results are influencing the company as a whole, you are doing everything possible to help your team members advance their skills. This kind of action will also keep you even-handed with the employees that you manage locally versus those who telecommute. This has the added benefit of ensuring there is no perception of favoritism or discriminatory behavior.

Later, you will learn how these kinds of managerial skills will also apply when you start your project management work.

CASE STUDY: PAUL SCHOEN

Paul Schoen is a project manager in Minnesota's Bureau of Criminal Apprehension. (This government organization is similar to the FBI but at the state level.) Paul offers that it is key to remember that there are soft skills and hard skills to management and project management. He offers the following:

"New managers should focus on building relationships first — the soft skills. Do not come to the position demanding that people 'tow the line' or similar behavior, no fist banging. As you build experience, you can ease into the harder skills where you demand people's accountability and such. But build your relationships at the onset."

Finding Your Own Managerial Style

When you stop to consider how many people attend colleges and universities in pursuit of a Masters of Business Administration (MBA), you might be tempted to conclude that these graduates must share the same opinion as to what management entails.

However, the opposite is true. It is almost like the field of medicine, in which we have so many specialties now that people seek out a work environment that matches their unique study or skills.

In the last section, we stressed how the primary focus is to keep your team's performance in your sights. But as you grow more comfortable in your role, you will notice there are different styles of management, just as there are different personality types. Some folks do well at 7 a.m., while others have energy peaks starting at 3 p.m. You will learn how to accomplish your goals in a way that works for you, as you hone your particular style.

Go to a search engine such as Google.com or Yahoo.com and do a search for "management styles." You will receive between 341,000 and 55 million results. You will find categories such as Management by Objectives, Management by Walking Around, Management by Exception, Management by Matrices, Management by Competitive Edge, Management by Consensus, and Management by Coaching and Development. If this were not enough, you then need to incorporate your personality into the mix. There are autocrats, democrats, controllers, plodders, motivators, and combinations of all the above. The scope of choices can be overwhelming if you are new in the arena.

First, your organization will help define your style. It is likely that your firm has measurement tools built into your performance appraisal. For instance, companies that believe in a value-added measurement as their bottom line will likely have predefined Management by Objectives goals for you to attain. You may have direction from your boss as you develop your own style.

As for the personality styles, we will explore some of these briefly so you learn to recognize that your team members also have their own styles. As part of your goal to develop your team, you need to recognize what kind of person each member is and work with that in the context of your company confines and goals.

Many people across the world have categorized managers. As we study the composite, we can derive four distinct styles, perhaps best categorized by Loren B. Belker and Gary S. Topchik in their popular book, *First Time Manager* as monopolizers, methodicals, motivators and mixers. Using their concept, we can present these four as follows:

1. The monpolizers may also be called Controllers. They insist upon taking charge of everything. They make decisions quickly. They are focused on the end result and don't care much to dwell upon detail. They are direct personalities who don't spend much time making "nice" talk or telling you about their families. They are not mean people, just focused upon the bottom line.

2. The methodicals are analytical. They are sometimes accused of "analysis paralysis." They take time to evaluate all possible data before deciding. They are the most careful of managers — the exact opposite of risk takers.

3. The motivators are creative, charismatic people who often have trouble completing what they start. These people are akin to cheerleaders. They may tend toward the Management by Walking Around style simply because they enjoy being near people. They are likely beloved by their direct reports. However, the Motivators struggle with the business side of things, the numbers, in particular. They do their best to make things happen, often based upon emotion.

4. The mixers are the politicians of Management. They are certainly dedicated and loyal to the company. They are equally patient and concerned about how people are doing. They try to balance the scales to avoid conflict and make everyone happy. They are the least likely to take a stance; they are true spin-doctors.

No matter which group you find yourself within, recognize another group — a subgroup. No matter if you are a cheerleader or analytical, you are also either a manager who expects your team to "obey your orders" or one who wants "consensus toward the ideas."

This is a difficult concept for new managers. Many people coming into management may fear a consensus style, for it may paint that you are "weak." Therefore, you may tend toward the barking orders approach and demand order and obedience. These sorts of managers believe that behaving thusly is the most efficient means to accomplish things, that engaging the "team" for input is only a waste of time and results in dissent. The other sort of manager — one who engages the team to understand the problem — hopes that the team will perform better because more people will better understand the problem. This manager wants the team members to feel as if they work "with" rather than "for" him or her.

Now that you have considered the various types of managerial profiles and how they interact with the subordinates, you need to consider the sorts of employees you will manage. Consider the following, as it relates to your people and controlling their results. Each person will require a different mix of control and encouragement from you:

1. Employee type one wants to do well but lacks skills. He or she will require constant evaluation and feedback and will reach out on her or his own accord. Evaluate/encourage this person using predefined measurements.

2. Employee type two is the classic "flatliner" who does what he or she needs to do before the end of the workday, then punches the clock and goes home. This person is heading toward burnout and will need much encouragement, above all else. Consider placing him or her as a temporary "in charge" if possible.

3. Employee type three is the "middle child" type. This person performs well and is no trouble. Therefore, she or he gets little attention. Don't overlook this person, even though it may seem as if little encouragement is required. The person still needs regular feedback. A possible "temp-up" position, as referred to in type two, may work wonders for this style of employee.

4. Employee type four is lackadaisical. This person seems despondent in that he or she has no evident desire to perform. This employee will require both your control and encouragement. It is likely that he or she is ready for either a new challenge or a new position. Try to place more demands upon him or her, if you can, such as adding a layer of new responsibilities. Otherwise, ask the person during your private review sessions what he or she wants to accomplish. It is the company to which you are most beholden, and although you do not wish to discount your employees, you can only lead them to "water" as the saying goes. It is up to them to drink.

5. Employee type five is someone who is at the end of his or her usefulness in the role. He or she is "burnt out" and is either ready to move on, at best, or ready to blow up, at worst. It is important to recognize this stage of a person's career and not allow it to spill onto others. The best scenario is when you can encourage your employee to seek a new position within the company. At worst, you may need to suggest that your employee move on, outside the company. This is the hardest type of situation that you will face as a manager. You'd best get prepared for it now because it will happen at some point in your career.

Learn to recognize the various personality styles and the type of motivation/control that each of your team members require. People skills are the biggest component of management and the most difficult.

As you progress through your career, read up on this complex topic. Psychiatrists and other professionals have devoted their entire lives to the study of how personality intersects with success.

What Is a Project Manager?

A project manager is a manager who is experienced in the skills and disciplines required to direct one or more projects at a time. He or she typically manages a team that executes the project. The project manager is responsible for overseeing the activity of the team members to ensure they track with the goals of the project.

What Is a Project, Exactly?

A project is a series of phases that comprises a life cycle, and when completed, brings a beneficial change that has:

1. A finite sequence of tasks that have a beginning and an end

2. An outcome that produces a unique product or service that did not exist before

3. A team of multidisciplinary people brought together who are clear about their expectations, why the project is necessary, what the expected goal is, and how the goal is to be achieved

4. A budget defining all resources such as cost, time, and head count

5. A deadline

6. A quality constraint well defined against a goal

7. A Scope of Work that is unique and considers uncertainty

What Is Project Management?

Project management is a methodology and a discipline that intends to bring benefits to its organization through such things as:

1. Managing complex change in an organized manner

2. Using prudent resources on the right projects

3. Tapping into the creativity and knowledge of carefully chosen team members

4. Setting quality objectives

How Is Project Management Deployed?

We will dissect the project in detail in Part 2, but for now, a quick overview of the elements of a project will be helpful.

1. A project contains segments, called "phases," that are deployed in sequence.

2. A phase contains actions, called "processes," that are deployed in sequence.

3. A project's beginning to end is referred to as its "life cycle."

It refers to the start of the first process of the first phase to the last process of the last phase.

THE PROCESSES, PHASES, & LIFE CYCLE OF A PROJECT				
Start				
Phase 1: Test Feasibility	Phase 2: Create Plan	Phase 3: Create Draft	Phase 4: Create Deliverable	Phase 5: Test & Release
Process 1 begins and ends; go to Process 2.	Process 1 begins and ends; go to Process 2.	Process 1 begins and ends; go to Process 2.	Process 1 begins and ends; go to Process 2.	Process 1 begins and ends; go to Process 2.
Process 2 begins and ends; go to Process 3.	Process 2 begins and ends; go to Process 3.	Process 2 begins and ends; go to Process 3.	Process 2 begins and ends; go to Process 3.	Process 2 begins and ends; go to Process 3.
Process 3 begins and ends; go to Process 4.	Process 3 begins and ends; go to Process 4.	Process 3 begins and ends; go to Process 4.	Process 3 begins and ends; go to Process 4.	Process 3 begins and ends; go to Process 4.
Process 4 begins and ends; go to Process 5.	Process 4 begins and ends; go to Process 5.	Process 4 begins and ends; go to Process 5.	Process 4 begins and ends; go to Process 5.	Process 4 begins and ends; go to Process 5.
Process 5 begins and ends; go to Phase 2.	Process 5 begins and ends; go to Phase 3.	Process 5 begins and ends; go to Phase 4.	Process 5 begins and ends; go to Phase 5.	Process 5 begins and ends; project is concluded.
				Finish

Why Use Project Management?

Standard, experience-based management methods are effective when performing jobs that can be handled by two or three people. But now, computers and automation have replaced many of the smaller tasks, leaving managers free to create bigger things. And with competition ever tightening, companies regularly challenge managers to make an impact that adds value to the entire department or even to the company itself.

To create change that promises this scope of value-added results, managers need to organize and engage people across many layers. A typical project team will comprised people of various ranks, from different departments, responsible for diverse functions. The project manager needs to keep multiple people consistently focused on the achievement of a common goal. He or she needs to manage the process so that everyone is tracking to a predetermined schedule and that the efforts are having the desired results.

As a new manager about to embark on a project, your initial opinion might be that project management is the answer to many challenges. The process might seem exciting and promising at first. You take the project home with you after work. You get excited over the many applications that you see. Soon, you have convinced yourself that you are going to single-handedly fix all the ills of your department.

But about two or three days into your study, you begin to see the scope of it all — in particular, the amount of planning that is required. You start to feel discouraged or overwhelmed before you begin. You might begin to wonder whether worksheets and a checklist are even productive. You might begin to think that you can accomplish the desired result without all the painstaking steps.

It is imperative that you do not fall into that trap. Recognize the competitive environment that American businesses face. There is a need for control and the willingness to abandon the project, if need be, if it is not working. The only way to do that — justifiably — is if you have established predefined conditions that say when to abandon it versus when to fix it.

If you try to manage a significant output by yourself, you stand to risk your own effectiveness at least. Plus, without a project management method, the sponsors who commission a project, the managers who oversee it, and the team members who work it might have different ideas about how things should be accomplished. It would be like an orchestra trying to perform a symphony without a conductor.

If you still doubt it, consider this example. A company that makes tires decides it needs a brochure that highlights the reasons it has the best quality products available in the United States today produced and disseminated among all its national stores.

The marketing manager assigned to this task calls her team together. She tells them the goal and says the following, "Juan, you write a brochure to explain why we are the best, and Kathy, you edit it. Chadora, you are in charge of making copies of it, and Leslie, you mail it out. The deadline is two weeks from Friday, so I need to see your progress this Thursday and again next Thursday."

In the above example, it is not out of the question that "something" will go out and the manager would have an opportunity to affect the final output, but consider that she put no expectations in front of her team. Neither did she exercise any cost comparisons. Who is her sponsor? Who is paying for this? What is her budget for each phase of it? What if Chadora disagrees with everything Juan wrote and wants to rewrite the whole thing? What size is the brochure? Standard, jumbo, fold-out, custom? Is she designing it in-house or out? What kinds of pictures will be in the final result? Who is the photographer? Does she want glossy or matte paper? Color or black and white? How will contractors be paid? What happens if there is a conflict in the pay schedule? Did she draw up a contract to address such occurrences? Similarly, what does the printing cost, in-house versus outsourced? Did she get quotes for that? Who is addressing the envelopes? What return address should the team use? How do they process returned mail? What kind of response tracking did the manager input? For instance, is there a promotion associated with this piece? A questionnaire? What means of tracking its effectiveness is built into the piece? Perhaps most important, what are the stores going to do when they receive this? What makes them care about it? Why should they not throw it in the trash? Is there some sort of contest associated with it?

This manager had a perfect opportunity to use project management for this task.

Please do not anticipate that just because someone above you says it is simple that it is. You need to educate your superiors, at times, and the best way to do so is to make recommendations about how to proceed. If you are given a task such as the tire brochure where you recognize that a project approach applies, recommend it to your boss. To support your point, you might compile a list of questions similar to the ones above and present your superior with this "reality check," along with a recommendation that a needs analysis be conducted.

If you get the go ahead, congratulations. If you do not, let it go. You might offer this suggestion up offhandedly with another manager in the organization, but beyond that, drop it. Unless you want to undertake serious office politics, that is about all you can expect for now. After all, your boss has the responsibility, ultimately, for his or her directions to you, just as you do for your team.

Now, let us suppose the opposite — that your queries produced a full-scale project.

Relax. Prepare yourself — and your company — for success. This is an opportunity for you to lead your team or a hybrid team of your people and a mix of others.

A good project manager will guide the project through a controlled set of actions to achieve the desired output. As a new manager in your company, you can use the tools presented in this book to demonstrate your leadership of time and resources. You will also discover opportunities to challenge your direct reports and assist them with their own career development.

Chapter 2

Preparing For Project Management

A new statistic indicates that fewer than half of all projects assigned to managers are completed, done correctly, finished on time, or under budget.

To protect yourself from falling into this group, you must plan. Planning is the best way to encourage success.

What are the Criteria for Success?

In almost all projects, success is defined by:

1. Finishing the project on schedule

2. Keeping expenses within budget

3. Meeting predefined quality goals

Experienced project managers cite a larger group of benchmarks that encourage success. Let us briefly look at them now. We will cover them again — and in more detail — as we walk through our project management practice.

1. Gain consensus and approval for the project.

In each phase of your project, it is imperative that you gain consensus and approval. Consensus means that you have proved the need to continue with the phase and that people are behind you. Equally critical, garnering approval will afford you resources, such as funding and people.

Warning: A project will fail without executive support.

2. Ensure that a feasibility study has been accomplished.

This is part of gaining consensus, but it is so important that it warrants its own focus. The feasibility study will contain quantifiable research that justifies whether the project is realistic. It should contain:

- Market analysis or work needs analysis that clearly substantiates the need

- Clearly described and defined risks and the key success measures

- Approximated costs to determine whether the organization or department can afford it

3. Build a winning team.

To identify the skills you will require, you will conduct a Work Breakdown Summary (WBS). We will cover this tool in more detail later. For now, realize that this tool will help you determine your necessary team members.

You will seek individuals who are deadline-focused, able to self-start, and who quickly grasp instruction. Personal traits such as patience and a sense of humor will not hurt either.

Warning: A project will fail if you select the wrong team members.

4. Develop a comprehensive plan and keep it updated.

This step is critical, and yet, many project managers either skip or skim this step. A common complaint is that there is no time to plan. It will come back at you if you do not create a written, detailed document that communicates the intentions, activities, resource requirements, and deadlines for the project.

Warning: A project will fail if you do not link all your activities to your strategy or if you are unable to explain why and how you plan to do every step.

5. Determine other mandatory resources required.

In addition to people and funding, you will need to consider both the internal and external resources you will require. If you are building a structure, for instance, you will want to plan for interviewing and evaluating contractors. Will you need electricians, plumbers, decorators? For how long and on what days? How much will each person cost?

This is another excellent use of the WBS tool. By stepping through each part of your project, you can then take the information you create here and apply it to your scheduling activity.

6. Create a realistic schedule.

A realistic schedule is a byproduct of a properly planned project. If you take the time to identify every resource and activity, you will be able to create a schedule that should track well. As you plan your schedule, allow for more time rather than less. While it may be tempting to show your sponsor that you can do it in miraculous time, you will lose your credibility if you fail to make deadlines.

7. Create attainable goals.

This benchmark is a natural extension of your normal managerial duties. You will pull together the data you have compiled so far (by the WBS and scheduling you have estimated) and begin to delegate to your team members.

8. Gain ongoing, written approval from management and stakeholders.

There are several steps built into the project that require you to stop and report to your sponsors, stakeholders, and other key people. Skipping these steps could mean you are acting without authority and even lead to disciplinary action. Make sure the people who need to give consensus and approval are tracking with you — and get it in writing.

9. Adapt frequently.

As your project progresses, you will undoubtedly need to adapt. Plan on things changing that will affect your data. Be prepared to kill your project, if need be. (We will address that in more detail later.) You might recommend changes to your sponsors as part of your regular feedback session. Stay flexible and be willing to try new things.

10. Motivate the team.

People normally resist change and become discouraged if their efforts continuously fail. When working a project, there will be many occasions when things do not go as you would like. As a manager, you will need to keep your team motivated. Your project's success depends on people. Do not overwork them. Do not demand the impossible. Do not lie to them about how things are going, even when it is extremely tempting to do so.

11. Communicate to stakeholders constantly.

In addition to the formal steps that require you to obtain consensus and approval and the steps that require you to give feedback, do not forget the power of the casual conversation. There is no reason you cannot mention various progress points to your sponsors as you encounter them during the day. Just make sure you do not use those occasions as reasons to skip the formal meetings with all the stakeholders and sponsors.

12. Review and close down.

At the end of your project, it will be tempting to put it behind you before you have closed it down, regardless of the outcome. But there are things you need to do to "wrap it up." Common tasks include writing letters of commendation to people who did exceptional work, returning all the goods you might have borrowed, paying all the outstanding bills, closing out any open contracts, documenting the results of the project, and making recommendations for the future.

What are the Skills for Success?

Many of the skills that are important in management are useful in project management, too. These are skills such as communication, leadership, delegation, persuasion, trust, team building, and conflict resolution.

CASE STUDY: CHRISTINA MAJEED

Christina Majeed is a project manager for NextTec Corporation, a medical software company. She handpicked her team and carefully considered the skills necessary for successful project management. She says the three top skills when seeking a person to work project management are that he or she is detail-oriented, has high energy, and maintains a positive attitude.

"As a project manager, you are detailed anyway, but you have time constraints. But if you have someone on your team who you can devote to the detail and has eagle eyes on everything, it will help. High energy is a must, and a positive attitude is very important. If something does not go as planned, think of it as an opportunity to make things better in the future.

"Other key skills include discipline; strong leadership skills; organization; time management; ability to be objective and take a step back from the situation, analyze, and decide how to fix issues. It does not hurt to have a little charm, too. After all, project management is all about getting things done. If people like you,

CASE STUDY: CHRISTINA MAJEED

see your passion and your ideas, they will resonate toward it and be more apt to help you.

"Finally, I also have observed that another trait that lends itself very well to both project management and management in general is the ability to self-analyze. Any manager who learns from his or her past mistakes as a means to acquire personal growth will find more success — both personally and professionally. "

CASE STUDY: SARY MABJISH

Sary Mabjish, a project manager in the pharmaceutical industry for the past four years, had this to offer about project management skills:

"In my case, the project manager first needs to be a people person. You will be dealing with different departments and different groups. For you to succeed and motivate other people, you need to be a people person.

"Even outside of the meeting, you are still working with people. Second, you need to have the knowledge. If you are well-versed and experienced in the project topic, fine. But sometimes we encounter things outside our full knowledge. You need to do your research and understand all the aspects of the projects and gain the background. If you do not have the knowledge, make your study very quickly. Third, you need attention to detail. Fourth, you need technical writing skills because this job involves writing and reviewing documents. Of course, you should have basic communication skills via phone, e-mail, meetings, or one-on-one. Be able to articulate effectively."

CASE STUDY: DAN MASON

Finally, Dan Mason offered interesting comments. Dan is a project manager at a real estate company in Florida. He is a cheerful person, and it comes through loud and clear over the phone.

"What skills do project managers need? Definitely confidence. Then organization, patience, and the ability to withhold your own frustration as you cheer on your team. Save your frustration for those Friday nights with your friends at the bar."

When considering the proficiencies you will need to master to be an effective project manager, realize that you are essentially managing people and non-people.

In the people group, you will find employees, managers, sponsors, vendors, bosses, and various support and contracted personnel. In the non-people group, you will find things such as time, emotion, health, education, and spirituality.

This is important because the manager who seeks to empower his or her team needs to be cognizant of the outside factors that come with each person. When planning a project, keep those extraneous items in your plans.

For instance, suppose you have a team of four people about to assist you on a project.

1. Barbara is a high-school graduate who spent 20 years raising her children and joined your company six months ago. She is self-motivated, has a strong work ethic, and likes working with others.

2. Henri joined the company two years ago. He is in his mid-20s and has a bachelor's degree in marketing. He is high-energy, on the go, a whiz at getting things done quickly but also quickly bored.

3. Marcus, who has been at the firm for ten years, uses a wheelchair. He has a two-year degree, is chatty, extremely flexible, and does not discourage easily, but he tends to take criticism personally and becomes angry when people do not express appreciation for his efforts.

4. Renee is four years away from retiring. She graduated college

25 years ago and has been with the company ever since. She knows practically everyone in all departments and is quick to tell people how things should be done.

If you were to put a schedule of activities together without considering each person's individual makeup, you would be doing the entire team a disservice. You cannot use Henri's time requirements as the team benchmark, for instance. Similarly, you cannot use Renee's knowledge of the company and expect it to apply to Barbara, who is on a learning curve.

Further, you should consider people's personal styles. In our example, Henri might get quickly annoyed with Renee. He is highly educated with a short attention span. Renee will certainly impose her advice on him, and he will have little patience for it. Marcus, by displaying a constant need for validation, might feel intimated by Henri. He might even express that by bossing Barbara around. With so much ego flying around, you should expect problems at some point — most likely on the day you roll out the third revision to your plan and it still does not work.

Consider that the true boss is the project. You need to keep your team focused on it by using your management skills, such as goal setting, delegation, and motivation. Remain aware that you will also need to manage "non-people" as you proceed.

The following provides a quick list of skills and behaviors that a successful project manager uses. Keep it handy during your project.

SEVEN SKILLS FOR SUCCESSFUL PROJECT MANAGEMENT

1. Focus on the project's outcome. The project manager will need to make decisions for the benefit of the project that some people will challenge. Listen to the challenge — the challenger might be right — but if you disagree, stick to your guns.

2. You manage; they do the technical work. While it might be tempting to do the technical work yourself, your job is to develop others. Assist them in doing their best possible work.

3. Deal with change; do not deny it. As part of your extensive planning, you will have done much to avoid many unexpected changes, but things will inevitably disrupt your plans. Admit it, address it, adapt for it, and advise your sponsor about it. Do not pretend it did not happen or gloss it over.

4. Make sure every member of your team understands all the ideas. A common pitfall for project managers is to spend more time developing ideas for the project than ensuring everyone understands what they are. Spend more time talking about the ideas than sketching them.

5. Expect conflict, crisis, and squabbles. Keep a cool head when dealing with conflict. Evaluate the situation and direct your team members as needed.

6. Use the Management by Walking Around style. Using this style of management during a project provides many benefits. It allows people frequent access to you if they have questions. You will also spot areas in which people might be struggling. It allows you to monitor people to ensure they are doing the tasks they need to do.

7. Communicate and motivate. By doing these things for your team, you will eliminate stumbling areas that much sooner and allow the team to achieve success that much sooner, and success is one of the greatest motivators of all.

Part 2

Identifying, Implementing, & Measuring Your Project's Actions

In Part 1, we examined the difference between a project and normal function. We described the qualities of a project. We defined management, project management, and a project. We analyzed managerial styles and skills that will help you succeed. You should now see how project management can be used to create a deliverable and why you would use it.

In this section, we will delve into how you will deploy a project. We will simulate a project by taking you through the entire process. In our example, we will use five generic phases to comprise our project life cycle. Finally, we will define and explore the project management process.

Chapter 3

Who Is Flying Your Plane?

A project's entire execution, from beginning to end, is called its life cycle. Within each life cycle are phases, and within each phase are processes.

How to Determine a Project's Phases

The phases of a project can take many forms. You need to use the ones that correlate to your particular industry whenever possible. Companies will either create their own or turn to professional resources for guidance.

For instance, several members of the PMI identified the development of standards and guidelines for major industries. The phases they recommend are found as part of the Project Management Body of Knowledge (PMBOK).

The *PMBOK Guide, Third Edition* is an internationally recognized work that sets the standards for project management. As part of its content, it provides the fundamentals of project management, by industry, that project managers may use as their guide. For instance, if you are in construction, the PMBOK suggests your phases are feasibility, planning and design, production, turnover, and startup. If you are in software development, the PMBOK suggests that your phases are concept cycle, first build cycle, second build cycle, and final build cycle.

The guide recognizes five basic process groups (phases) that we will use throughout this work and incorporate into our examples. These are listed as follows:

Five Generic Phases of Project Management

- Initiating

- Planning

- Executing

- Controlling and monitoring

- Closing

Within each phase, the PMBOK defines the interaction between phases and processes. Much of the science of project management is derived from this work and can be summarized as follows:

Phase I, Initiating: Demonstrate the Need or Feasibility

- Examine your organization's guidelines, policies, bylaws, and culture.

- Gather historical data to find out if similar projects were undertaken and what lessons were learned.

- Conduct a market analysis to confirm that your project is feasible.

- Conduct a Statement of Work and obtain approval from your sponsor.

- Create your initial preliminary Scope Statement.

- Execute the project charter, which defines your roles and grants you permission to continue.

- Move to the second phase.

Phase II: Create the Project Plan

- Conduct a series of steps that will ultimately produce your project plan, such as:

  ° Activities required

  ° Resources required

  ° Schedule

  ° Costs

  ° Assumptions about deliverables and constraints

  ° Obtaining consensus and moving to the next phase

Phase III, Executing: Create Specifications or Draft of the Deliverables

- Further define each deliverable.

- Process requested changes that happen as part of your feedback.

- Take corrective action, if required.

- Obtain consensus and approval and move to the next phase.

Phase IV, Controlling and Monitoring: Create Deliverables

- Fine-tune the definition of each deliverable.

- Approve or reject change requests.

- Approve corrective or preventive actions.

- Update the project management plan.

- Update the project Scope Statement.

- Create performance reports.

- Approve deliverables and move to the next phase.

Phase V, Closing: Test-Market, Release the Deliverables to Market

- Administrative closure process

- Contract closure

- Final product rollout

Now let us look at the process to begin, implement, and conclude each phase. This is where the heart of your work will be.

Putting Processes and Phases Together

The way you will begin a project is by first doing a work-needs analysis or some similar kind of report to substantiate the need for the project. You will create a document that describes your intentions and expected costs and present it to your sponsor. The sponsor is not only the person (or people) who will pay for the project — he or she is your client.

The phases of your project will take you through this process systematically. In our example, you will initiate Phase I, Determine the Need or Feasibility. Apply the first step of Process I, Get Your Project and Phase Authorized.

After you have authorization, you will begin your planning session. You and your team will work hard on this process. There will be many activities conducted in the planning stage. When you complete it, you will bring your findings to your sponsors and stakeholders to discuss your results and then close the planning process. During that same meeting, you will seek authorization and consensus to begin the next process — Execution.

This cycle continues. You execute your plans and then evaluate them carefully to maintain careful control measures. You may launch your product or service in stages and make adaptations based on how the limited release models perform. When you are finally satisfied with your execution, you will conduct the final process stage and close out your project.

Michael Greer offers a detailed description of the combined interaction of processes and phases quite effectively in his work, *The Manager's Pocket Guide to Project Management*. We took his work and built upon it to create a cookbook style of instruction for new managers. The following is an interpretation of his work and the PMBOK data, showing how the two functions interrelate, from start to finish.

PROJECT PHASES AND PROCESSES COMBINED	
Phase I: Feasibility	**Activities: Initiate, Plan, Execute, Control, Close**
1. Demonstrate Project Need & Feasibility	• Create a document to substantiate a need for the project. Outline and describe the expected deliverables. Explain the means, the costs, and the costs of the deliverables. Highlight the benefits to be obtained.
Obtain Project Authorization	• The sponsor authorizes or declines. • Authorizations are put into place that allow you (as project manager) to obtain resources and other items of support you will require.

PROJECT PHASES AND PROCESSES COMBINED	
Obtain Phase Authorization	• The sponsor will review the objectives you have defined for the phase and decide to approve organization resources such as funding, people, and time to the activities of the phase. . This is distributed as the Project Charter.
Phase II: Plan	Activities: Initiate, Plan, Execute, Control, Close
2. Describe Project's Scope	• Create a schedule by using Gantt charts, network diagrams, work breakdown studies, milestone charts, or text tables. • Compile supporting details, such as resource usage by week and costs.
Define & Cycle Project Activities	• Create a list of activities that will be performed on the project. • Update your charts as necessary (WBS, network diagrams).
Estimate Time Each Activity Requires & Resources Needed	• Break down time required, by activity, and list your assumptions for each estimate. • Describe the resources you will require and why.
Develop Initial Schedule	• Break down time required for each activity and when each resource will be required. • Create an initial calendar.
Estimate Costs	• Estimate costs for completing each activity, including supporting data. • Describe how to handle cost variances.
Build a Budget & Spending Plan	• A cost-based spending plan tells how much will be spent on what resources, at what time.
Organize & Acquire Staff	• Define the roles and responsibilities of each assignment. • Create an organizational chart.
Close Out Planning and/or Adapt	• Confirm project plan has received written approval from the sponsor. • Obtain approval to begin work on the project.

PROJECT PHASES AND PROCESSES COMBINED

Revisit the Project Plan & Adapt	• Create a document describing potential risks, why you fear them, and your recommendations to address them.
Phase III: Create Draft	**Activities: Initiate, Plan, Execute, Control, Close**
3. Quantify Terms for Deliverables	• Deliverables are created, possibly in stages. • Necessary changes are identified.
Phase IV: Create Deliverables	**Activities: Initiate, Plan, Execute, Control, Close**
4. Create the Deliverables	• Decide to accept inspected deliverables. • Make corrective actions. • Update your project plan and Scope Statement.
Phase V: Test & Implement	**Activities: Initiate, Plan, Execute, Control, Close**
5. Test & Implement Deliverables	• Obtain formal acceptance, documented in writing, that the sponsor has accepted the product. • Update contractor's files. • Update project records and prepare for archiving.

Chapter 4

Systems Check

In this chapter, we will step through the actual experience of managing a project at a high (summary) level. We want you to see the end-to-end process in its entirety. Then, in the next chapter, we will begin to pull together the actual documents you will use to accomplish the deliverable and let you see the detail.

For our simulated project, you have identified a need that exists in your department to create an employee handbook. You manage an entry-level group of people, and as such, there is habitual turnover in your group. Conditions regularly exist in which one person is covering for someone else who has been promoted or has resigned or simply helping to train somebody new.

Your team of 25 people supports nearly 200 salespeople in five states. You are one regional team out of four nationally. (The remaining three regions have the identical organizational structure.)

The members of your team create sales brochures, process marketing letters, research databases for requested information, pull sales reports, budget spending reports, and compile similar reports for sales people and sales managers. They also do miscellaneous typing, scanning, and mail duty. Your team also consists of the secretary to the vice president of the region. This person keeps his calendar, answers his phone, processes his mail, and runs errands at his request.

Early in your new assignment, you recognize that many of your team members do not know what the other members do. Worse, they do not care. There is a feeling among many that the secretary is given special treatment, even though she is the same rank as most of the others, because she is the secretary to "the big boss." No one goes out of the way to help her much, even though she is willing to lend a hand to others when she can.

As a new manager, you are trying to gain an understanding of everyone's roles and frequently find yourself asking whomever you can about various practices. Some members will do their best to answer you, and others quickly reveal their "baggage" to you in their replies, such as, "That is not my job," or "You will have to ask so-and-so."

You have two vacancies to fill and another person scheduled for maternity leave in three weeks' time. You start to make a list of every person and individual roles and responsibilities so you can figure out where to begin to organize your team. Suddenly, a brilliant idea occurs to you. Would it not be better to have each person detail in writing his or her own job, and then share that information with the others?

The possibilities and the applications for such an undertaking begin to ignite within you:

1. The document will be a resource for your team.

2. It will provide answers to virtually anyone about how to get something done.

3. It will allow people to become cross-trained with minimum effort.

4. It will be an excellent tool for new hires as they master their learning curves.

5. It will help with describing a position for future advertising, when vacant.

6. It will help stay the costs of turnover to the department.

7. It will be a way for the group to work on something together.

8. It will help the team members learn new skills.

9. It will possibly help the team members advance their careers.

10. It will be something that your division could roll out to the other three divisions.

At this point, if you are an average manager, you are excited by these possibilities.

Before you go rushing off to your boss to get permission to do a project, do an analysis. First, verify this is a project and not a part of your normal duties. Ask yourself the key questions:

- Is it a finite sequence of tasks that have a beginning and an end?

- Will it produce a unique product or service that has not existed before?

- Will I require a team of multidisciplinary people brought together who are clear about their expectations, why the project is necessary, what the expected goal is, and how the goal is to be achieved?

- Will my managers and sponsors expect me to create a budget defining all resources needed for such an undertaking, such as cost, time, and head count?

- Will there be a deadline required to get this accomplished?

- Will my managers and sponsors expect to see a quality constraint well defined against a goal?

- Will I need to create a Scope of Work that is unique and considers uncertainty?

Since you are able to answer these questions affirmatively, it is safe to proceed.

Next, determine whether you have identified the correct sponsor. Consider that the sponsor will be paying for the endeavor. You are assuming that your sponsor is the vice president. Consider all the options before you are certain, such as:

- Is he financially and organizationally aligned to you and able to provide the support you need? In some instances, you may want to seek someone external to your division. The bottom line is that you need to ensure the person who is authorizing the project is at a high enough level to authorize and fund the project.

If the answer is no, ask yourself who else you need to include in your target audience as you pitch your idea. It could be that you will need to address your idea to more than one sponsor. Think this through carefully.

If you determine that a different sponsor or additional sponsors are required, ask yourself how you will engage those people. Use your own boss, whenever feasible, to guide you.

Phase I: Demonstrate Project Need and Feasibility

Initiate Phase I

Create Document that Demonstrates Need

The first thing you will do is prepare a written document confirming a need for the deliverable you intend to produce. You describe, at a high level, why you are doing it (based on your analysis), and you identify the major activity levels you expect will be necessary. You include an approximation of the costs to create and implement the deliverable, such as the people, funding, and time that will be required. You quantify the benefits of the deliverable also. For example: You compute the total number of days that any positions have been vacant for as long as you have records (five years is more than enough) and, using an average salary, quantify how much it costs the department every day to support a vacancy.

Make certain to express your core project clearly and concisely. Include all the goals you wish to accomplish. Associate them with their costs, risks, and benefits. The purpose of your project is to create something beneficial to the company. Be sure you are able to quantify and prove this as your intended result as you present your facts during this stage.

Be sure to include your costs and benefits analysis for the project in your recommendation. Provide substantial detail about your strategy. You want your sponsor to have a keen awareness of what he is getting into.

Practice your presentation before a mirror. Many managers do not do this, but this simple exercise can set you apart from mediocrity. It could suffice to simply read it aloud at your desk, but by adding a mirror to the mix, you will see the little things that will help you make your presentation that much more effective. You might have the soundest reasons on earth for your project, but if your material does not present well, you will negatively affect attitudes of key decision makers.

Presentation skills should be considered carefully. A big part of effective management is the ability to make highly effective presentations. There are several avenues available to you to hone this skill, such as:

1. Look at what your local community college has to offer. It normally has affordable evening classes that address ways to enhance communication skills.

2. The Web has countless articles on this subject. A particularly helpful article posted on the **Inc.com** Web site can be found at the link: **www.inc.com/guides/growth/23032.html**. This article is interactive in that it has several links within it that supply you with additional information or tips about effective communication.

3. You local library will have self-help books and tapes for you to check out.

4. There are clubs dedicated expressly to this purpose, such as Toastmasters International. You can find your local chapter at the link: **www.toastmasters.org**.

In addition to presentation skills, it will benefit you to hone your writing skills. The written word conveys a wide scope of information, emotion, and persuasion. Simply being able to communicate your message clearly and concisely will put you ahead of the pack.

When you have completed your needs analysis, you want to ensure you have addressed these key items:

- Did you identify the correct sponsor who can support all the financial and organizational needs of this project?

- Did you clearly define the project without using jargon or other language the sponsor might not understand?

- Does your needs analysis clearly substantiate the project?

- Did you include a clear and detailed cost and benefits report about the project?

- Did you include all items that the project will entail — the good and the bad — so the sponsors will fully see what they are getting into?

Plan Phase I

Obtain Authorization from the Sponsor

You receive the decision from your sponsor to either proceed or abandon your plans. If the project is a "no go," you shelve it. If it is a "not yet," set up a reminder in your calendar to revisit it at the interval that your sponsor requested.

If you get a "go" decision, you are off and running. The first step is to create the project charter. This is a document that formally recognizes the project. It announces you as the project manager and authorizes you to obtain resources. The goal of the charter is to demonstrate that the project has the support of upper management and to encourage people to support you.

Most project management books will describe a project charter as something written by upper management. While this can happen, the process of creating the project charter is varied. Some project managers write them, and others have their sponsors write them. If you find your sponsor will write it, you still want to ensure it contains critical items. Because whether you write it or someone else does, there are key elements to a project charter that need to be included.

- The scope of the project — what you will and will not work on

- The deliverable(s) you intend to produce

- The objectives and success criteria

- Your expected schedule, cost, and quality constraints

- Primary stakeholders and roles

- Key assumptions

- Risks and/or obstacles and how you plan to address them

CASE STUDY: DAN MASON

Dan Mason had been a project manager for almost two years when his firm's president distributed this letter to announce the first project that Dan managed. You will see how it announces the key facts about the project, but the underlying, strong message is that the employees need to support the project manager to their fullest potential.

Dan comments that when he first received the letter, he carried it with him like a weapon. "I thought it yielded a lot of power. I was new a new manager and had not yet established myself in the pecking order. I was prepared to whip out the letter and flash it like a badge if anyone challenged my authority." He laughed and continued, "I soon learned that the letter is nowhere near as important as the confidence that you demonstrate. That, plus the respect you give others. Those two character traits together are more powerful than any letter. But still, it does not hurt to have your project announced by the big cheese."

The project charter next reflects a real-world example, provided by Dan Mason. The names and dates have been changed to reflect our project.

THE PROJECT CHARTER

Date: May 4, 2008

From: The Big Cheese
           President, Southeastern Sales Division

To: Managers of Project Team Members (Listed by Name)

Cc: Project Team Members (Listed by Name)
           Key Region Managers (Listed by Name)

Effective May 4, 2008, Daniel Mason will be the Project Manager of the employee handbook project. Daniel will continue to support (His Manager) during the duration of the project.

As sponsor of this project, I am committed to its success. I authorize Daniel to issue direction in matters relating to the project. Further, Daniel has my support to obtain any resources necessary toward achieving its objectives. You will find additional detail about Daniel's responsibilities in the attachment.

Although your direct report(s) will continue to support you during their project assignments, I will expect that they apply their primary focus to the success of the project. As such, they will be expected to fully communicate with Daniel about any scheduling issue that will result in a missed deadline or other issue that will threaten the project's success.

I know I can rely on you and your team(s) to fully cooperate with Daniel on the project. We anticipate the employee handbook will be available for employees by the end of June.

Please join me in welcoming Daniel to this assignment.

(Signed)

Mr. Cheese

Attachment

Page 1 of 2

THE PROJECT CHARTER

Overview of Daniel Mason's Responsibilities as Project Manager in Handbook Project

Planning Phase:

1. Sanctioned to schedule cross-functional team members to work on project, as required

2. Sanctioned to direct team members to create an attainable project schedule

3. Sanctioned to pull team members into weekly meetings

4. Sanctioned to negotiate contracts with outside vendors, provided terms are within budget

5. Sanctioned to assign action items to team members and to resolve any resulting schedule conflicts with cross-functional managers to fulfill project's requirements

6. Required to bring sponsor out-of-bound conditions such as major risks to costs, schedule, or scope, along with recommendations

Execution Phase:

1. Sanctioned to assign activities to team members and to request status from them to ensure major milestones are obtained

2. Responsible for ensuring all items are held to schedule, including escalating as needed. This includes outside vendor commitments as well as internal commitments

3. Required to bring sponsor out-of-bound conditions such as major risks to costs, schedule, or scope, along with recommendations

Delivery and Closeout Phase:

1. Responsible to test, gather feedback on trial release, and relay results to sponsor

2. Expected to draft a summary of findings and recommendations

3. Responsible for written performance evaluations of each team member

Page 2 of 2

CASE STUDY: SARY MABJISH

If you find that you are responsible for creating your own charter, you may want to follow the example of Sary Mabjish. He explains how he generates and uses the charter:

"At the beginning of a project, the team members and the project manager write the charter, route it through the team first, then on to the stakeholders.

"Do not start the project prior to getting the charter signed off on. If you start the project and do not have the support from upper management and later on you run into issues, upper management will have something that will take priority over your project.

"I initiate a project with the charter document. We specify the scope of the project, the departments involved, the stakeholders, the time lines, the budget, and a very important section called the constraints. For example, suppose that for this product to succeed, we have to have the approval of the budget, or five people dedicated on this project only, or we have to have certain things done in a certain sequence. We specify those conditions in the constraints section. Then, this document routes first for the team leader and the team to sign, then to the primary stakeholders to sign so that everyone is in agreement.

"Suppose that later on the amount of the budget is cut back. We are able to show the direct effect, and in our status report, we state something like, 'Because the budget was not approved, the scope of the project was going to be this, and now it will have to be condensed because we do not have the costs allocated that we needed.' Or, if we do not have the manpower, the time line will change. We will state, 'Instead of four months, it will take six or seven.' During the project, when things change, we do not abandon the project; things will change. You need to track them, modify, and get sign-off to their impact."

CASE STUDY: BOB ECKERT

Bob Eckert is a project manager who has led IT infrastructure projects for more than 17 years and has been a senior systems integrator for the last nine years. He believes that the charter is one of the leading indices of the project's success. He states:

"You have to start the project with a charter. It is so important to understand

CASE STUDY: BOB ECKERT

what it is you are trying to deliver and whom you can work with to get it delivered. Stakeholder management is so important. Imagine if you tried to build a house without involving the city inspector, and eventually the inspector showed up and saw that you had not met code for a particular component of your house. Think of how much time and money would be spent to comply with the city code. Many projects include the stakeholders too late or not at all."

Execute Phase I

The execution of this phase is simple. The project charter, upon its dissemination, has effectively executed your phase. By its nature, it also grants you approval to continue.

Building Your Team

The next thing you should consider is choosing your team.

CASE STUDY: BINH VO

Binh Vo has been involved in project management for ten years. In his experience, he has held roles as varied as doing tasks for the project as well as fully managing them.

He is currently doing project management as part of his overall duties for a company in Florida, and we asked him to share some of his tips. Along with those came "reality checks." Here is one.

"If you are just starting out in project management, you probably will not have the opportunity to pick your own team. In the real world, the team is decided for you, with the possible exception of giving your opinion about what outside contractor agency to use."

If circumstances allow you to pick your own staff, follow these rules:

1. Consider what competencies you will require.

2. Write a job description.

3. Talk with your human resources person to make sure you follow the correct processes to "borrow" employees from other departments, do not cross pay scale or union guidelines, and understand how to interview without breaking any laws.

4. Consider people you have worked with in the past and whether any of them might be a fit — or available — for your project.

5. Create a skills inventory of people in your own organization. List their technological, managerial, administrative, and human skills. Compare their skills to the competencies you require.

Note: Do not expect to find a 100 percent match of skills available to 100 percent of the competencies you require. If you are seeking people who are "thick-skinned," for instance, and one of the people in your group is "thick-skinned," he or she qualifies. Move on down the list and see if you obtain the list of people you want — and their skills — not by one person but by a culmination.

If you are unable to find enough people in this exercise, you will need to consider alternatives, such as training any existing employees who are available for the project in the skills you require or seeking candidates from outside the company.

CASE STUDY: PAUL SCHOEN

Paul Schoen has had experience in both selecting his own team and having them assigned to him. He explains:

"I have had projects where the team members are assigned and times when I can pick my own. If you

CASE STUDY: PAUL SCHOEN

are a project manager starting out, it does not really matter how you acquire your team members, as long as you have the ability to establish relationships within your field of work and within your company. If I have a sponsor who says, 'Here are my thoughts about what we need to do. We will have some challenges in areas, and you are confident with people in the departments where we will need some help.' This is where you will write the business case. In our setting, we have to justify and identify resources to get it done. Even before you begin any detailed work plan, or identify the specific deliverables, consider whom you might need. For instance, 'two business analysts, an architect, a tester, and co-project manager, because I am going on vacation for a month.'

"With regard to putting together a team, always ask yourself what you are doing. Is your deliverable to produce a paper report about a product or the actual product itself? Or are you building a system to code software to build an application? If I need a business analyst, I look for someone who has done business analysis. I look at their experience, the quality of their work, and the timeliness of their work because I know that if I have a great business analyst, they will keep everything in check. And beyond that, I look for people who will be responsible and accept accountability for the quality of their output."

It is easier to train an existing employee than to hire someone new. Hiring an outside person will mean training them in the project and about the company. Existing employees are also a known entity.

Sometimes you will work a project that requires you to communicate with team members around the world. The skill set for such a project may also include multilinguistic capabilities.

CASE STUDY: MIKE HEUTMAKER

Mike Heutmaker has worked as a project manager for five years for Digi International out of Minneapolis, Minnesota. Prior to that, he was a project engineer for another eight years. Consider what Mike has to say:

"Within the teams I have worked, there has typically been a resource pool to draw from. Certain team members are 'always' assigned to a specific product group, i.e., an embedded technology team.

CASE STUDY: MIKE HEUTMAKER

"Teams are defined at the onset of a project by the engineering managers, based on skill set and availability. At our company, this could consist of hardware and software teams and production facilities that are scattered around the world. Our current team members include hardware engineers from Minnesota and Germany and software engineers from Minnesota, Boston, Germany, and Spain. The product will be built in Germany and then shipped to Minnesota for packaging and shipping to customers. So as you can see, efforts from many different global locations are required to make a project a success. The skill sets are not only technical but organizational, too."

The "Volunteered" Team Members

As we stated, it is more likely that you will have your team volunteered to you by other managers in your organization. People can be selected for good and not-so-good reasons.

In a perfect world, a manager will provide you with one of his or her direct reports because the person has the types of skills you are seeking. More likely, the person is simply available. Worse, it is because he or she is expendable.

It might be easy to get discouraged if you receive a mix of people and some are "non-producers." Before you slink away in despair, consider the following:

1. The change you are bringing to this person's life might be welcome. It is common that someone who is not performing at top levels in his or her normal position can show marked improvement when given a project. It might be boredom with the daily grind, dissatisfaction with his or her direct supervisor, or that the skills required on the normal job are not the person's greatest asset. Do not assume the worst before giving the person a chance.

2. You will likely need to build training into your project, even if everyone on your team is top rated.

CASE STUDY: SARY MABJISH

Sary Mabjish comments about having a team delivered to you versus picking one:

"Depending on the project, I prefer to pick the subject matter expert because he or she will give us the most input. If that person is not available, I next try to pick the supervisor. For us to proceed with the project, you have to have some kind of influence to affect the work, and if you cannot get the subject matter expert, try to get the manager."

Put Benchmarks and Rewards in Place

No matter who ends up on your team, be sure to develop a performance and recognition system as part of your project. Provide your members with performance reports at regular intervals so they will have an opportunity to address any action items, and be sure to tell people when they are doing well as often as you see it occur.

Control and Close Phase I

Depending on your industry, in some cases, you will group two or more processes together. In this instance, your control process involves the ongoing, careful selection of your team members as quickly as you can obtain them. During the kick-off meeting, you will have the following objectives:

1. Present a thorough overview of the project and expected deliverable(s).

2. Introduce each team member and his or her respective role.

3. Obtain commitment from each team member that he or she will complete the assigned activities on time and within budget. Some project managers have a contract they pass around and have everyone sign. This action is more definite, for many people, than a mere verbal commitment.

4. Ask each team member whether he or she has what is needed for the project. If not, make a note of what each needs and get it. If the team members tell you that they need something that you are not sure is necessary, engage them in a dialog, but keep yourself at the lead. For instance, if someone is responsible for writing how the word processors type the sales letters, and that person tells you she needs a new computer to do her job, find out about that. Maybe the computer is actually broken, or maybe it is a ploy to try to get an upgrade when it is not necessary. The goal is to make sure everyone knows you will get them what they need for the project.

5. Provide a written authorization to each team member to begin work on his or her individual activities, and copy that person's direct manager. Be as specific as necessary in this memo, such as what times you will expect that person to report or when the major deadlines are for milestones.

At this point, Phase I is complete, and you move on.

Chapter 5

Choose a Runway

Concurrent with the onset of Phase II are the activities in the planning process.

The scope of tasks you will complete in Phase II will require the greatest amount of time during the project. This is by design. Do not try to skip over tasks in this phase — you will only increase your chances of failure.

Because there are so many activities requiring data gathering, extrapolating, and planning, we will divide Phase II into two separate chapters. In this chapter, we will describe the tasks necessary to create a Scope of Work Statement and begin the following project activities:

1. Create a Work Breakdown Structure.

2. Create an activity list.

3. Create a network diagram.

4. Estimate the duration of each activity.

5. Assign resources to each activity and prepare initial schedule.

6. Create a project schedule and its associated Gantt chart.

7. Estimate the costs associated with each activity.

In Chapter 6, we will use the data we create in Chapter 5 and continue with our project's activities:

8. Create a budget for each resource.

9. Create a variance plan.

10. Establish the quality constraints.

11. Create a communications plan.

12. Create a risk management plan.

13. Create the project plan, based upon all the above.

There is a rule known as the 1:10:100 Rule that is important to know. It applies whenever you create or develop anything new. It has been tested and verified across virtually every industry, from construction to medicine. The rule is this: It is least costly to plan thoroughly and resolve problems in the planning stage. It costs 10 times more to resolve the same issue in the building stage and 100 times as much when it gets into production.

CASE STUDY: BINH VO

Binh Vo corroborates how careful planning not only drives a more successful project, but how it is also a true time saver:

"One of the biggest ways to save time during the project management process is to plan well.

"Think about this: If you had an activity on your list to go to the grocery store and buy things for a party, would it be faster if you went directly to where you needed things or went down every aisle, looking for your items? Sitting down ahead of time and making that list will save you time and give you the opportunity to make sure everything is on the list. Validating your shopping list with items is like validating your requirements with users."

Phase II: Create the Project Plan (Part One)

Initiate Phase II

Obtain Authorization for the Phase

Your first item is to seek authorization for the phase. Your sponsor (and other managers as required by your company) will authorize you to use the resources you need to begin.

When obtained, you ensure that all stakeholders are also advised of your project by circulating the project's information to internal and external stakeholders, as required.

Note: External stakeholders are often vendors. For instance, if the company that produces your award trophies is frustrated because it is not receiving orders in time to make the product, let it know you are giving their concern a full review to identify the root of the problem and meet the interval requirements.

Plan, Execute, and Control Phase II

In the planning process, you will execute a series of documents that will control how the project is deployed. In this instance, planning is grouped with executing and control.

Although there are numerous steps involved, it is simply a matter of answering these basic questions:

1. What needs to be done?

2. How will it be done?

3. Who will do it?

4. When will it begin?

5. When must it be completed?

6. How much will it cost?

7. How good does it need to be?

Because the bulk of Phase II is spent in the planning (executing and controlling) mode, we will provide you with a series of actions, and beneath each action will be the associated steps. This will be annotated as action number, step number, abbreviated as A1:S1.

By following all the steps, end to end, you will gain a thorough scope of a well-executed planning phase.

Describe the Project's Scope

Action 1: Create a Work Breakdown Structure

The project scope is defined as a high-level description of everything to be included and excluded. Its composition will also suggest the size of your project. As you do more projects in the course of your career, you will learn that assessing the project scope is one of the first things you will consider. Project managers have different measurements to define a project as small or large. Some say anything that lasts more than a year is large, less than six months is small, and in between is medium. The industry as a whole tends to consider projects with 30 or fewer activities to be simple in scope. Others have thousands of activities. Consider the project to build an amusement park, for instance.

Next are the steps to follow to complete your scope definition:

1. Develop a Work Breakdown Structure (WBS) that includes

every person or function affecting the project.

2. Define the problems to be resolved by the deliverables you will produce.

3. Quantify your major objectives, such as cost, schedule, and quality criteria.

4. Develop a project strategy.

5. Write a Scope Statement to define the boundaries of what you will do and what you will not do in your project.

A1:S1. Develop a Work Breakdown Structure. Project managers often will begin this phase of the project by defining the deliverables. We are not going to start there for a couple of reasons.

First, we believe that when your sponsor told you what you were to deliver, you would have asked enough questions to understand exactly what you would be creating. This is an important notion that will be stressed throughout this work. Therefore, we are making the assumption, which we will later verify, that you already clearly understand what the deliverable looks like, in detail.

Therefore, we are going to begin this activity by going directly to the Work Breakdown Structure. This tool will allow you to "visualize" all the components of your scope. From there, it is a natural progression to hone in on each deliverable. In our exercise, we are creating an employee handbook. We begin by describing the functions.

For instance, consider the secretary to the vice president's position. She answers his phone, keeps his calendar, processes his mail, types his sensitive memos, and does light errands as part of her duties. The word processors receive internal requests from other employees to type customer proposals and letters. They might also receive requests from management to help them prepare a sales report. The data support person is responsible to order all new cell phones, handhelds, computers, and computer-related hardware for the Information Technology (IT) department. The operations support person is accountable for pulling sales and budget reports and working with the operations manager to make sure all the data there is accurate.

Our WBS would look much like the one shown in Figure 5-1.

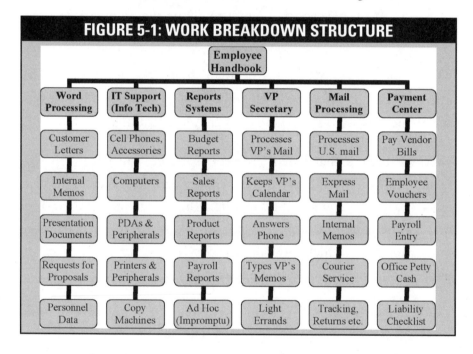

FIGURE 5-1: WORK BREAKDOWN STRUCTURE

A1:S2. Define the problems your deliverables will resolve. Recall that you answered many of these questions when you prepared the need and feasibility document. Now, you and your team should spend ten or 15 minutes "brainstorming" about every problem that is happening because of problems such as vacancies and no cross-training. Be careful, because these kinds of exercises tend to turn into "gripe" sessions. Keep people focused. When you are done, your list might contain things such as "had to postpone my vacation" and "sales reports are not always done on time." This is your list of problems that your deliverables will resolve. Now, turn it around and list your deliverables.

- Deliverable: The employee handbook that contains detailed instructions about every function that the support team executes

- Deliverable: A description about word processing customer letters

- Deliverable: A description about word processing sales reports

- Deliverable: A description of who services the word processing machines

- Deliverable: A description about how to obtain toner for the printer

- Deliverable: A statement about how we will accept change requests as we work on the project

- Deliverable: A statement about how we will communicate our status with the sponsor and the stakeholders

- Deliverable: A schedule of when we expect to have the project completed

- Deliverable: An expected date when a first draft will be ready for review

Keep going until you list everything you and your team will create.

A1:S3. Quantify your major objectives. In this step, you will specify your on-time and budget criteria. You will decide the date that your project will begin and approximate the end date.

So far, you have mapped out every function that you plan to describe in the employee handbook. You also have defined the deliverables you intend to produce. The final component you need to consider is your quality measurements. Consider such things as, "We will work on this project without disrupting someone's regular work schedule," and you will define any out-of-bound conditions that may lead to a change in scope or threaten your intended deliverable such as, "If Employee Z is not available to explain the payroll process, we cannot continue since Employee Z has all the expertise."

Once you have this information defined, take a step back and ask the team how long it will take to finish the project. By defining your start date, Scope of Work, intended deliverables, and out-of-bound/quality constraints, you should have a good idea how long the project will take.

You will find that many sponsors will set your schedules for you. It is common for a sponsor, who is also a high-level manager, to say something such as, "I want a new car designed by September 30 of this year, and here are your specifications." We will address this more when we discuss scheduling, but for now, remember that it is your job to ensure that your sponsor's desired deliverable is realistic. As such, it is critical that you take the time to identify all components and deliverables and work with your team to schedule each activity.

The next step is to extrapolate your costs and scheduling at the onset. Again, the costs were already something you considered when you conducted the feasibility study. In this instance, you have the advantage that you manage the support staff; therefore, you have data available to tell you the range of costs, from paper to personnel.

If you work a project where you do not have this information, you will do some research by calling the people who do know. For instance, if you were managing a project set to deploy a new software package, you would contact the IT manager and ask him or her about costs to deploy similar software in the past.

There are several ways to estimate costs that will be explained in the next chapter. For now, be aware that the most common is known as bottom-up estimating, which means that you estimate the cost of each element of the project, then add them together.

A1:S4. Develop a project strategy. You will do a broad-brush description of your communication plan, explaining how you will handle out-of-bound conditions, how you will manage risks and constraints, and any addressing assumptions that correlate to your management plan.

1. **Communication plan.** The importance of an effective communication plan cannot be overstated. Without a clear and timely communication plan, people will be more apt to lose their accountability and blame others. It is especially important to implement a clear-cut and easily accessible plan if you have remotely located team members.

   At this step, you need to identify the type of medium and processes that you plan to use for communications. Later, you will create a highly detailed plan with your team.

2. **Risks and constraints.** Similarly, you will identify the key item that will trigger an out-of-bound condition and thereby jeopardize the project. You will mention how you will manage these situations.

For instance, you will want to include a statement about how you will manage "scope creep" in this section. This is the process of gradually adding work to a project, after it has begun, until your original cost and schedule projections are useless.

3. **Other assumptions.** You will list any remaining assumptions that you used as part of your plan, including the resources you will require.

You will also include a chain of command indicating the project's reporting structure. Projects are matrix organizations, meaning that the people on your team will likely report to someone else in another department for their day-to-day duties but to you for the project. Said another way, their functional management structure is their normal daily environment, and by working for you on just the project, they are within a matrix environment. This is important because you want to make sure you are working in concert with the person's functional manager. With this in mind, you will want to create a written responsibility table that defines each person's major roles and responsibilities. Be sure to identify who will manage and maintain the project file. An example of a matrix flow is found in figure 5-2.

It may be tempting to skip this step, but do not. This tool addresses decision-making and authority roles up front. You want to avoid situations where you are at odds with another manager in the organization over who is supposed to direct the employee and when.

FIGURE 5-2: MATRIX FLOW

Name	Function	Project Function	Reports To	Expected Need Dates
Laura	Sales Reports			
Henri	Sales Reports			
Daniel*	Budget Reports			
Arturo	Mailroom			
Joe	Mailroom			
Marcus	Pay Center			
Carla	Pay Center			
Elena	Word Processing			
Renee	Word Processing			
Vacant	Word Processing			
Barbara	VP Secretary			
Kris	IT Support			
* new hire effective 6-23				

A1:S5. Create your Scope of Work Statement. You will organize the information you produced in your previous work into a single, comprehensive document known as the Scope Statement. You will deliver this report to the sponsor and the key stakeholders for concurrence and sign-off. Be certain to define what you will not do in the project, as well as what you will do, to ensure everyone has a clear expectation of the end product you will produce.

An example of a Scope Statement is found below.

THE PROJECT SCOPE STATEMENT

PROJECT DEFINITION: SCOPE OF WORK

Project Name: SUPPORT STAFF EMPLOYEE HANDBOOK

1. Project Background and Justification

The clerical staff exists to support people who bring in revenue to the company. As such, these support people need to have every level of training available to them as well as every resource that they require to ensure they perform at the highest possible level.

THE PROJECT SCOPE STATEMENT

In the past five years, the vacancy rate of the Central Region support staff is 30 percent on average. This equates to three to four vacancies out of the 12 positions available. This constant shortage is due to regular turnover. The nature of the position is entry level; therefore, many people are promoted, laterally transfer, or are dismissed due to performance issues. The impact on the other staff members is that they are required to cover for vacant seats nearly 1/3 of the time. The impact on the sales members is that they need to wait longer for items they require to either manage their business or support their customers. It is not possible to extrapolate the potential loss in sales with a good degree of accuracy — however, it is not providing a positive effect.

2. Project Objective

To minimize the impact of vacancy, this project seeks to create a means to cross-train each support clerk so that he or she can provide assistance across more areas than just his or her primary function. A key product that will assist in that attainment is to create and maintain the support staff employee handbook. The project team intends to create this objective in-house within a six-week interval, concluding by June 30, 2008. We will use the support staff as the primary resource and will use the tools that already exist as part of company business, such as word processing machines, copy machines, and distribution systems. We will purchase resources only as needed, such as extra paper, toner, and binders. The total cost for people and resources is an estimated $10,000.

3. Primary Stakeholders and Their Roles / Responsibilities (including customers, sponsors, reviewers, contributors, and project managers)

   a. Customers are the Central Region sales team, support staff, and managers. They are responsible for providing input to the project team about items brought to them. For instance, the sales manager(s) may be given a draft of a description to review and asked his or her opinion about how it reads, or a manager may be included in a brainstorming session to contribute ideas on how a process flow could be enhanced. Not every employee is a stakeholder, but every employee is a customer. The project manager will differentiate.

   b. Sponsor is the Central Region Sales Vice President

   c. Reviewers are:

THE PROJECT SCOPE STATEMENT

- Sponsor, who decides action when major risks to cost, schedule, or scope of the project are identified to him by the project manager

- Stakeholders, who participate in milestone meetings and offer feedback

- Team members who work the project, evaluate, and offer feedback

d. Contributors are:

- Support staff team (List by Name)

- Project manager (Your Name)

- Experts, both internal and external, as defined by project team, for input

- Resources, such as trainers or training materials, and software

e. Project manager is responsible for leading the team through all phases of the project: initiate plan, execute, control, and close. Responsibilities include creating the project schedule; allocating the project budget; assessing risks; conducting team meetings; negotiating contracts with outside vendors, providing terms of the contract are within the pre-approved budget; assigning actions to team members and working with their respective managers to resolve time conflicts; requesting status so that milestones are on track; identifying key problems to sponsor, such as change in scope, schedule, cost, or quality and making recommendations; and providing written feedback to project team members.

4. Project Deliverables

The primary deliverable is the employee handbook. This reference material will describe every function the support staff performs. When a vacant condition arises, any member of the support team can step in to assist. Offshoots of this deliverable will be to stem job boredom and broaden the skill set of each person.

A streamlined version of this tool will be distributed to the sales people to use as a reference. This version will omit sensitive data, such as passwords for access into restricted areas. However, by sharing the infrastructural processes, the sales people will be better able to manage their own business. They will be

THE PROJECT SCOPE STATEMENT

able to identify such things as when the cutoff time is for overnight deliveries, what the standard interval is to word process a Request for Proposal of 250 to 500 words, or how to order customer brochures.

5. Project Milestones

In the course of the project, there are four key milestones identified, so far. First, it is expected that Version 1 of the document will be composed by May 30. Second, Version 2 is expected by June 10. Third, an updated list of cost, schedule, or scope changes as seen at the midpoint of the project is expected by June 16. Finally, Version 3 is expected by June 30 for a limited, test rollout.

6. Key Assumptions

The project will produce a handbook describing the support staff's functions. It will be a quality document, produced in-house, and copied double-sided onto white bond paper. The handbook will not describe any other job function, such as sales people's. The support staff will continue to meet its regular work demands during the project. There is no authorized overtime. These job descriptions will not replace the HR descriptions required to advertise vacancies. The handbook will be completed within six weeks and will cost $10,000 or less.

Action 2: Define the Project's Activities and Succession (Activity List)

1. Create a list of each activity to be performed in the project. Research historical information for these same activities that might have been performed on other projects for reference data.

2. List each activity's natural work flow, from start to finish, and assign an estimated time element to each one.

A2:S1. Create an activity/task list. A typical project is composed of a series of tasks. Each task should either equal a deliverable or be part of a deliverable. For instance, we saw in Action 1, Step 1 that one of the deliverables is a description about word processing customer letters. The associated task, therefore, will be to write a job description for the word processor staff detailing how to process customer letters.

Note that throughout this work, we will use the term "activity" to be equal to the term "task." Note that in project management, a task normally defines a sub-activity, a job that is too minor to be included in the first level of detail in a WBS. But since our project is simple, our activities themselves will be basic; therefore, we are comfortable in using task and activity interchangeably.

Each task needs to represent enough work to warrant its own action. It should have a clear deliverable but still be short enough to track its progress regularly and identify problems early. Tasks are defined as requiring either hours or days worth of work.

Many new project managers will question why it is necessary to create such a painstaking itemization of tasks required. There are two main reasons for this. First, you want to be certain you have all necessary steps accounted for. Second, you will then apply estimated costs to each activity. This will comprise your cost estimate, and later, your budget. Therefore, be certain to encourage your team to brainstorm for every step required in the project.

CASE STUDY: CHRISTINA MAJEED

Christina Majeed stresses the importance of inviting the team to bring up ideas.

"I have excellent team members. Everybody has ideas. And they bring them because they know they are welcome to bring them. When people start to roll, expressing their ideas freely, it becomes a true brainstorm session with lots of good thoughts coming to the table. Plus, when people are heard, it makes them want to be part of the team that much more.

"I believe that one of the things about being a good leader is to recognize that other people have good ideas, other than yourself. As a manager, you have the ability and the power to put ideas into action, and you want to put the best ideas into action. If one of your team members has a great idea that you put into action, you make them look good, and you look good."

For our project, you might expect that most activities will center on word processing, since we are creating a document. But as you and your team have a brainstorming session to list all the major pieces of your work, you will uncover many other activities besides typing. Your initial list may look like:

1. Talk with others who may have done a similar project to gain their input.

2. Consider whether there is historical data that will help ensure you have all the necessary activities identified. For instance, in a sales department, you may tap into the experience of the sales managers as they responded to a client's request for proposal (RFP). Often, an RFP is a lengthy, detailed document that involves the input of two or more sales people, plus their manager, to produce.

3. Seek the input from an expert in the field of the work. Even if there is no one else in your division who has comprised

an employee handbook, look for someone else who has. You might find someone after hours at the health club, at church, or at a club you attend. Ask your team to seek out this individual, too. Do not be afraid to look for the input of someone who has already done a similar project to yours. Even one tip from this person might save you time or money as you complete your own.

4. Interview each person to ensure you capture a firm understanding of his or her function.

5. Gather examples of the output that each person produces, when appropriate.

6. Inquire about resources that each person relies upon.

7. Type the descriptions.

8. Meet as a project team to evaluate progress and predict costs, time to complete, associated budget, and quality constraints.

9. Have another person or people edit the typing for errors and content.

10. Revise the document.

11. Meet again, as in step #8.

12. Meet with stakeholders and sponsors to advise of progress and challenges.

13. Revise again, as necessary.

14. Copy the document.

15. Order necessary materials for output, such as extra paper, toner, person hours, or binders.

16. Final editing.

17. Bind, as necessary (staple, laminate, hole punch, as required).

18. Distribute the document to a small, controlled audience.

19. Use the document.

20. Update it for flaws or omissions.

21. Meet as a project team to discuss necessary revisions.

22. Decide what extra costs may be required for revisions, if not initially budgeted.

23. Distribute updated version.

24. Update it for changes to roles or as required.

25. Final distribution.

A2:S2. List each activity's natural work flow, from start to finish, and assign an estimated time element to each one. This exercise will allow you to think through which steps you must do first. For instance, when you first comprised your activity list, "order supplies" was down as Task 15. But as you think through which tasks depend on previous tasks, you realize you will need to order supplies before you copy the handbook. Certainly, you will need paper, toner, and binders, for instance, to copy the work. So you move that task up on the list toward the start of the project.

You want to continue this process until you have completed all the tasks in the project, the estimated duration of each task applied to your calendar, and the first pass through at which resource will manage each task. You will have an output similar to Figure 5-3, when you are completed.

Once you and your team believe you have a good grasp on the project's required activities, from start to finish, you need to group them. One of the best tools available for this exercise is to use a network diagram, which we will create out of the effort we put forth by creating the activity list, as shown in Figure 5-3.

FIGURE 5-3: ACTIVITY LIST: EMPLOYEE HANDBOOK

FIGURE 5-3: ACTIVITY LIST: EMPLOYEE HANDBOOK

ID	Task Name	ID	Task Name
1	Talk with other project members.	24	Version 1: Document
2	Consider historical data.	25	Meet with team again.
3	Seek input from an expert.	26	Meet with sponsors, stakeholders.
4	Interview each person.	27	Revise.
5	Interview IT support.	28	Final proofread
6	Interview word processors.	29	Copy document.
7	Interview report clerks.	30	Bind document.
8	Interview mail processors.	31	Version 2: Document
9	Interview payment clerks.	32	Controlled rollout
10	Interview VP secretary.	33	Test the document.
11	Gather examples for each function.	34	Hold project team meeting.
12	Gather resource information.	35	Costs, revisions, etc.
13	Hold project team meeting.	36	Meet with sponsor for OK.
14	Order materials.	37	Update the document.
15	Paper	38	Revise.
16	Binders	39	Type revised version.
17	Toner	40	Proofread.
18	Dividers	41	Version 3: Document
19	Postage	42	Copy document.
20	Misc., i.e.lunch, sodas	43	Bind document
21	Type initial descriptons.	44	Final distribution
22	Edit.	45	Close project.
23	Revise.		

Action 3: Create the Network Diagram

1. Create your project's network diagram to show how the activities relate to each other — which ones are dependent on others or are products of others.

2. Evaluate and make any necessary revisions.

A3:S1. Create your project's network diagram. Once you have identified the tasks that are dependent on others, you can draw a network diagram. A network diagram will allow you to see the relationships between activities and to group them or modify them, as necessary.

The first thing to do is to look for precedents in your activity list. A precedent is something that must happen in order for the next task to happen. For instance, will talking with another project member produce historical data? No. So, step one is not a precedent to step two. Is considering historical data going to produce input from an expert? No. So, again, step two is not precedent to step three.

However, it is certainly necessary to interview the members before you type their job descriptions, or to type the document before you copy it.

By identifying precedents, you will be able to clarify your activity work flow and create your network diagram. Our initial network diagram would look like Figure 5-4, below.

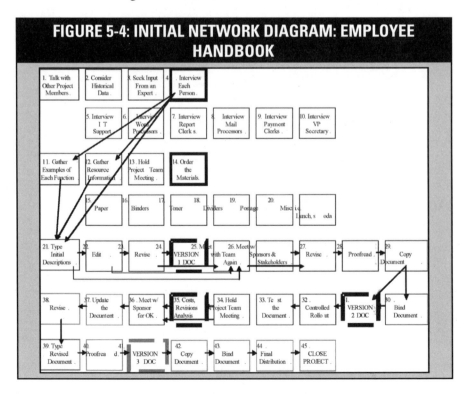

FIGURE 5-4: INITIAL NETWORK DIAGRAM: EMPLOYEE HANDBOOK

A3:S2. Evaluate and make any necessary revisions. Now it is time to take a step back and look over your data. Do you need to break down some of your tasks into subtasks? Do you need to split some of your tasks if you see they will be interrupted and need to resume later in the schedule? Are any of your tasks recurring?

Upon review, you decide that task four, Interview Each Person, needs to be broken into smaller tasks. You decide to create subtasks, as shown below. After that, you feel satisfied that you have a good baseline of tasks and your best-estimated duration.

Action 4: Estimate the Duration of Each Activity

1. Compose a list of available resources and their associated functions.

2. Comprise a worksheet indicating each activity and its expected duration.

3. Group activities that go together and update the network diagram.

A4:S1. Compose a list of available resources and their functions. In this example, you have the advantage of being both the functional manager and the project manager. Therefore, you have the list of each resource person and his or her associated function handy, as shown in Figure 5-5.

FIGURE 5-5: RESOURCES AND THEIR FUNCTIONS

Resource	Function
Manager	Management
Barbara	VP Secretary
Marcus	Pay Center
Laura	Reports
Arturo	Mailroom
Joe	Mailroom
Elena	Word Processing
Renee	Word Processing
Henri	Reports
Kris	IT Support
Daniel	Reports
Carla	Pay Center

A4:S2. Comprise a worksheet indicating each activity and its expected duration. You are beginning to put together the initial schedule for the project. As such, you decide you will take the first pass at evaluating each item and its associated duration. You also decide that you want to start your project soon, so you begin to put some framework around the calendar.

1. You decide to do the first task yourself and speak to the other people who may have done a similar project in the past. You decide you can accomplish this in half a day and assign yourself to it on the project start date of May 19.

2. You also decide to use Kris for other research work, since she will be leaving. You assign her the task of researching historical data that contained activities similar to this project. You will give her a couple of suggestions, such as the RFPs that may have been compiled previously, perhaps

training documents that the HR department wrote or the compensation plan that headquarters may have generated. You will as also add this research to the list of items to brainstorm, when the team comes together.

3. The heart of the project goes to interviewing each person and capturing the key elements of his or her job. For this activity, you elect to create a committee of sorts and assign three people — Barbara, Marcus, and Laura — to do the interviews. You believe this will ensure that if one set of ears misses a point, the other two will catch it. You also make this decision to encourage Barbara to learn about the other functions, since she is so focused in her role of VP secretary, and to encourage the cross-training culture that you expect will be a byproduct of the project.

4. Along with the interviews, the project requires that each person submit "examples" of his or her work to be included in the final deliverable, along with a complete disclosure of resources required. For instance, the mailroom will submit a completed copy of a DHL, FedEx, and USPS overnight label, indicating all the appropriate codes to charge correctly. Along with that example, Arturo and Joe will provide the contact information for each company, such as local office address and phone numbers, office hours, Web site, and the like. You elect to give this task to Carla, as a check and balance against the work that Barbara, Marcus, and Laura are doing in their interviews.

5. After the project team meeting where all the initial information will be shared and discussed, you will ask Carla to order the necessary materials to create the final deliverable. Copy paper, toner, binders, and shipping

materials are part of the list. You will expect the team to brainstorm to include all the necessary materials for this activity during the meeting.

6. You will also ask Carla to find out the company's rules about ordering materials or resources outside the normal work process. For instance, if the list of required materials exceeds $500, what threshold of approval is required in the company? You will look to Carla to identify those details for you.

7. You will assign Elena and Renee to type the interview from the notes that Barbara, Marcus, and Laura provide. You have to be cognizant of the normal word processing demands, so you are careful not to schedule an entire day for the project.

8. You decide that Henri will read the first draft aloud to find areas where the sentence flow is awkward. You also expect him to look for typographical errors that the word processing automatic spell check might have missed. For instance, in a sentence such as, "To print checks, load them in the printer so that the checks are facing upwards and you signature line is at the top," a spell checking system will not alert you that the sentence should read "your signature," not "you signature."

9. Henri gives his corrections back to Elena and Renee. When they make the updates, you have created a first draft and reached a milestone in your project.

10. You will meet with your team to review the results and discuss challenges and potential problems. You will discuss the remaining steps in the project and ask your team to

comment about any concerns.

11. You will take the first draft and any concerns to the sponsors and stakeholders for their input. Assuming the project is still authorized, you will continue with your activity list.

12. You will make any revisions that came about from your team, as well as from your sponsors' and stakeholders' input. You will pass those revisions to Elena and Renee and direct them to repeat the edit cycle.

13. Upon their completion, you expect them to give the printed, revised document to Henri. He will edit and proofread again and return any comments to Elena and Renee.

14. This time, when the document is corrected and printed, you will instruct Arturo and Henri to make copies for your team, bind it as if it were completed, and distribute the finished product to each team member. This is another milestone in the project. You have conducted a controlled rollout, and the team will now test the document for the next three days.

15. You will ask the team members to switch roles during this period and use the document to determine how to accomplish the task.

16. You will pull your team together again to discuss how the swap of duties worked. Where were there problems, and where was the book most effective? You will take that feedback and create the next set of revisions.

17. If the next set of revisions will require expenses beyond what you had anticipated, you will need to evaluate them

carefully. Perhaps the copy machine is not functioning properly and jams so much that your people are tied up twice as long as you had anticipated. What is the cost of outsourcing the copy job? You may need to assign someone on the team to research this question for answers.

18. You will meet with the sponsors and stakeholders to provide an overview of what is working and what is not, along with your recommendations.

19. Assuming your project is still a go, you decide to make yourself accountable for the final revisions, based upon input from the team and your sponsors. You give the changes to Elena and Renee.

20. They make the changes and give it to Henri for proofing.

21. Arturo makes the final copies and Henri assists him (or they deliver it to an outside copy source).

22. Joe takes the copies and binds them; Henri assists him (or they deliver it to an outside office supply source).

23. Arturo and Joe deliver the final deliverable to all appropriate people.

24. You spend a day closing the project.

After you take the time to think the project through to the level of detail above, you feel confident about your initial assignment of resources. You load it onto the calendar and produce the table shown in Figure 5-6.

FIGURE 5-6: ACTIVITIES LIST AND EXPECTED DURATION

ID	Task Name	Duration	Start	Finish
1	Talk with other project members.	0.5 days	5/19/08	5/19/08
2	Consider historical data.	0.5 days	5/19/08	5/19/08
3	Seek input from an expert.	0.5 days	5/20/08	5/20/08
4	Interview each person.	3.5 days	5/20/08	5/23/08
5	Gather output examples for book.	3.5 days	5/20/08	5/23/08
6	Ask details person's resources.	3.5 days	5/20/08	5/23/08
7	Hold Project team meeting.	0.5 hrs	5/26/08	5/26/08
8	Order materials.	0.5 hrs	5/26/08	5/26/08
9	Type initial descriptons.	2 days	5/26/08	5/27/08
10	Edit.	1 day	5/28/08	5/28/08
11	Revise.	2 days	5/29/08	5/30/08
12	Meet with team again.	0.5 hrs	6/2/08	6/2/08
13	Meet with sonsors, stakeholders.	1 hr	6/2/08	6/2/08
14	Revise.	2.5 days	6/2/08	6/4/08
15	Final proofread.	1.5 days	6/5/08	6/6/08
16	Copy document.	1 day	6/9/08	6/9/08
17	Copy document.	1 day	6/10/08	6/10/08
18	Bind document.	0.5 days	6/10/08	6/10/08
19	Controlled rollout.	0.5 days	6/11/08	6/11/08
20	Test the document.	2.5 days	6/11/08	6/13/08
21	Hold Project team meeting.	2 hrs	6/16/08	6/16/08
22	Costs, revisions, etc.	0 hrs	6/16/08	6/16/08
23	Meet with sponsor for OK.	1 hr	6/17/08	6/17/08
24	Update the document.	3 days	6/18/08	6/20/08
25	Revise.	1 day	6/23/08	6/23/08
26	Type revised version.	1.5 days	6/24/08	6/25/08
27	Proofread.	0.5 days	6/25/08	6/25/08
28	Copy document.	1 day	6/26/08	6/26/08
29	Bind document.	1 day	6/27/08	6/27/08
30	Final distribution .	0.5 days	6/30/08	6/30/08
31	Close project.	0.5 days	6/30/08	6/30/08

A4:S3. Group activities that go together. As a final step to Action 4, give your network diagram another look. Are there any activities that go together? Ask yourself whether the person who works on one activity will, by default, be working on another. If you are satisfied that there is no need to modify it any more, you are ready to go to the next step. Otherwise, you want to update the network diagram.

Action 5: Assign Resources to Each Activity and Prepare the Schedule

1. Review your organizational calendar and people's schedules to identify what days are not workdays. Double check any days that a team member will not be available.

2. Create a list of assumptions or constraints.

3. Assign resources.

A5:S1. Review your organizational calendar and people's schedules to find non-workdays. Once you obtain schedule information, you need to project the data onto a calendar. This calendar is one that you will continuously update throughout the project. There are any number of choices:

1. A plain, paper calendar on which you enter data with a pen or pencil

2. A calendar from a software system, such as ACT® or Microsoft Outlook®

3. Project Management-specific software such as Microsoft Project®

Note: If you expect to do several projects throughout the year, you would be wise to use project management-specific software. We will discuss various software options in Part 3.

When you obtain your group's schedules, you recall that Kris, the IT support clerk, is scheduled for maternity leave beginning on June 2. You will want to gather all the information from her before May 30, and you do not want to schedule her to work on any activities in June. You also know that you have a new hire coming in as of June 23 to fill the budget-reporting vacancy.

You log that Kris is unavailable for all of June, Barbara is off on May 29 and 30, Marcus is off the week of June 16-20 and Daniel is scheduled to begin June 23.

The work you do around this activity is the base work for both your schedule and your budget. Although you first steps are simply to gather data about people's availability, it is important to see the big picture. You are getting ready to assign people to tasks. Do not assume an eight-hour day. People rarely work a full eight hours, unless they are robots.

CASE STUDY: BINH VO

Here is a good tip that Binh Vo uses when he puts his schedule together:

"Scheduling is one of the biggest challenges. I recommend that you build it by consensus. You have to understand all the activities and talk to the people who do the activities and ask them how long it will take.

"When you speak to these resources, pretend they are machines that never have to eat, sleep, etc. and all they do is work, work, work and they can start work and do all the work until it is completed. Listen to their input, and then add up how many hours they tell you it will take, then divide that by six. Use six as a realistic full work day. After all, every few hours, people will take a break, or they will talk socially or sometimes go home early. Use six hours as your work day and three hours as a half work day. Many seasoned project managers already know this; it is what I would laughingly call 'One of the dark secrets of project management.' Use this as a benchmark, but do not tell them this."

A5:S2. Create a list of assumptions or constraints. As you work toward putting together the schedule, there are some things you will need to assume. In the tip that Binh Vo offers, above, he suggests that we assume a six-hour work day instead of an eight-hour day for the reasons he states. Perhaps that will be one of your assumptions. It is important to review and include any assumption or constraint that will limit the project.

Note that an assumption is defined as a decision that the project team applies to the planning. A constraint is a restriction that is imposed on the project by the organization or from outside the organization that limits what the project must achieve, how, by when, and at what cost. As you consider the possible items that may arise to limit or test your project, be aware of both of these factors.

As you considered your work so far, you assumed you would be able to begin soon, so you targeted May 19 as your start date. You also assumed that you would be completed by June 28; therefore, you do not want to schedule any activity beyond that date. You will want to set your sponsor's expectation that you can complete this project in about six weeks, as was your assumption.

You need to be aware of a commonly used project management calculation that is applied to calculate the schedule durations. The technique is called Program Evaluation and Review Technique (PERT) and it employs three estimates (best, least, and most likely) to describe the range of an activity's span of time.

Many people use the PERT chart as a network diagram, but a PERT chart uses probability factors to calculate its output. Still, the PERT diagram is widely in demand today because it not only depicts the activities, but it also shows how each is connected, with a line (known as an arc), and it highlights the critical path, too. You are more likely to find it built into project management software than network diagrams.

You need to understand the concept of the critical path; it is key in project management. The critical path is the sequence of activities in a project that take the longest time to complete and thereby determines the minimum schedule for a project. The project manager keeps an eye on the critical path because every activity must be completed on time or the project will overrun its schedule. However, there is more to it.

In order to perform successful scheduling, it is vital that you understand key concepts that are used by project managers, as follows:

1. Early Start (ES) refers to the earliest time any activity may be started. It accounts for any precedents, in particular.

2. Late Start (LS) refers to the latest time any activity may be started and still complete within the schedule.

3. Early Finish (EF) refers to the earliest time any activity may be completed. It typically describes the best case scenario such as everything going right and perhaps includes additional resources to help with various components of the activity, known as Fast-Tracking.

4. Late Finish (LF) refers to the latest time any activity may be finished and still complete within the schedule.

5. Float, sometimes referred to as slack describes the amount of time that any task can be delayed without causing a setback to either subsequent tasks or the project's overall completion date. Therefore, you can see how float is a desirable thing to see in a path. If there is no float, it means that there is no time buffer and each activity has the same Early Start / Late Start and Early Finish / Late Finish times.

   i. Free Float (FF) refers to the time required for an activity to complete and not delay the finish of any successor activity. In order to calculate free float, you subtract the earliest start time from the latest start time, shown as a formula LS − ES = FF.

ii. Total Float (TF) refers to the cumulative time required for all activities to occur and not delay the termination date of the project. In order to calculate total float, you subtract the earliest finish time from the latest finish time, shown as formula LF − EF = TF.

iii. Negative Float (NF) refers to the state at which all the float is used up and the project will be late.

6. An activity without float is considered critical, and a total path without float is known as the critical path. The project manager keeps an eye on the critical path because every activity on it must be completed as scheduled or the project will overrun its timeline.

There are several popular techniques used in project management that allow you to calculate the duration of each activity and ultimately, your schedule.

1. The Forward Pass method. This method reveals each activity's earliest start and finish time and its critical path. It is derived by adding the early start to the first activity's duration to reveal the early finish of that activity. Then, the next activity is added to the first number and so on for each activity, successively. The outcome is considered one possible timeline for your schedule. The formula for Forward Pass is shown as:

2. The Backward Pass method. This method reveals the latest start and finish time that can occur without missing your

activity and project deadlines. It is derived by taking the last activity's duration and, working backward, subtracking the succeeding duration from the early finish

For example, suppose you have a project called Walk the Dog to the Corner Store to Buy Him a Toy. You decide you want to walk your dog to the corner market to buy to him a toy – and maybe something for you too – then walk him back. How long would that take you to do, using the Forward Pass method? You need to start breaking this down by activities.

First, you have to make sure any precedents are completed. Suppose your dog was out with your spouse, at the vet. You cannot begin the walk until he returns home. So, we assume all the precedents are met.

- Activity 1: You call your dog and he responds to you right away. You put on his collar and fasten the leash. This entire process takes one minute. This now becomes the Early Finish (EF) number for the Activity Call Dog and Attach Leash.

- Activity 2: You exit the house and walk down to the corner store in 15 minutes. The Duration for the Activity Walk to Store = 15. The EF for this activity = 16 which is the sum of the first activity plus the duration of this one.

- Activity 3: While you are walking, you consider the various toys that you might buy for your dog. You recall that he likes the flying discs and you decide that toy is your first choice. You consider other toys while you are walking in case they are out of discs, and you have your choices made within 5 minutes. The duration for Activity Consider Toys to Buy

= 5 and the EF = 6, which is the sum of the first activity and the duration of this one. You will notice that the EF for this activity is less than in Activity 2, even though they are being done concurrently. This is normal because most activities that are done concurrently do not have the same duration.

- Activity 4: You go inside and look at the toys. You discover there are at least three choices of flying discs so you consider them. You finally select a cloth, waterproof disc and head toward the register. You notice the store is selling ice cream cones and you decide to buy one for yourself. You pay for the ice cream cone and the dog. The entire process takes 12 minutes. The duration for Go Inside, Buy Toy & Ice Cream = 12. Now you need to compute the project's running EF. Do you add this duration to the 6 minute EF derived from Activity 3 or the 16 minute EF derived in Activity 2? The answer is that you always use the longer of the two numbers, so that your schedule has the best chance of being met. So, you will add this duration of 12 to the EF of 16 to get a new EF of 28.

- Activity 5: You walk home and the duration for Walk Home from Store is 15, the same amount of time as walking there. The EF for the project now becomes 43.

- Activity 6: While you walk home, you eat the ice cream. The duration for Eat Ice Cream is 5 minutes, shorter than the duration for Walk Home from Store. Again, we add the larger duration of simultaneous activities to the previous EF and we compute our new EF of 43.

- Activity 7: You return to the house and remove the leash,

open the bag, show the toy to your dog, remove the wrap, and toss the disc to him. The EF for Go Inside and Give Toy to Dog = 2. The total EF for the project Walk the Dog to the Corner Store to Buy Him a Toy = 45.

The above example used Forward Pass to calculate the total duration of the project's earliest start and finish times. Now, let's use Backward Pass computations to reveal the latest possible start and finish times that can happen without destroying your timeline. The difference between these two calculations will reveal the float.

LS and LF values are obtained by starting at the last activity and working backward, subtracting the duration of the preceding activity from the early finish of the activity.

Starting with the project's overall EF = 45, you would compute as follows:

- Activity 7: 45 – 2 = 43. 43 is the LS for Activity 7.

- Activity 6: 43 – 5 = 38 but Activities 5 and 6 are concurrent, so,

- Activity 5: 43 – 15 = 28. Which number do we use when we move to the next bullet as our LS? When using Backward Pass, that number would be the smaller of the two as it will give you the least amount of time, which is what you need to budget for. In this instance, we would use 28, therefore.

- Activity 4: 28 – 12 = 16.

- Activity 3: 16 – 15 = 1 but Activities 2 and 3 are concurrent, so,

- Activity 2: 16 – 5 = 11.

- Activity 1: 1-1 = 0.

When you analyze the amount of time allotted for each activity using forward pass and compare it to the time for that same activity using backward pass, you are deriving the float for each activity. If the number is 0, that means there is no float, or no leeway in your activity and you must watch these activities especially closely. These are the critical paths of your project.

If the number is negative, you have identified negative float and you should adjust your activity's durations at once.

Figure 5-7 is a visual of all the concepts we have explained in this section.

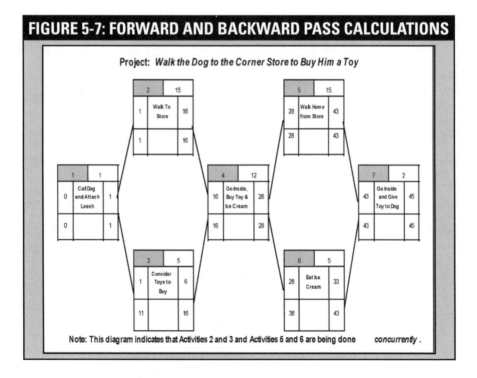

FIGURE 5-7: FORWARD AND BACKWARD PASS CALCULATIONS

Project: *Walk the Dog to the Corner Store to Buy Him a Toy*

Note: This diagram indicates that Activities 2 and 3 and Activities 5 and 6 are being done   concurrently.

FIGURE 5-7: FORWARD AND BACKWARD PASS CALCULATIONS

ACT	DUR	ES	EF	LS	LF	FF	TF	
1	1	0	1	0	1	0	0	CRITICAL
2	15	1	16	1	16	0	0	CRITICAL
3	5	1	6	11	16	10	10	
4	12	16	28	16	28	0	0	CRITICAL
5	15	28	43	28	43	0	0	CRITICAL
6	5	28	33	38	43	10	10	
7	2	43	45	43	45	0	0	CRITICAL

Now you are about to assign resources to the activity list. You did your due diligence along the way, accounting for people who will not be here and assuming that the ones scheduled to report will be here. Should you assume that, however? You are not leaving any room for possible illnesses or other unexpected vacancies. Perhaps you need to build extra time into your project. You will need to consider those kinds of items as you work toward building your planning.

A5:S3. Assign resources. You are now ready to assign the people to the activities. In addition to the dates when people will be off work, you will want to consider any heavy work loads they have pending.

If sales reports are always due at a certain time each month, you do not want to assign multiple tasks to the people who have to pull reports that will be necessary for paying the sales people on their results. You should consider each person's individual traits, ability to handle work loads, and who works more slowly than others. Although you want to make sure you do not overload the people who do well to compensate, you do need to take advantage of the most efficient. It is a balancing game that you will need to play.

Finally, you will want to consider people's salaries when you get through the first schedule together. You will have a budget for this project, and part of it will tie directly to how much you will pay personnel.

If you lay a heavy load of activities on the highest-ranking, highest-paid person, you will need to ensure your budget will support it. In our example, after you have considered all the above, you produce the table as shown in Figure 5-8.

FIGURE 5-8: ACTIVITIES RESOURCE ALLOCATION

ID	Task Name	Duration	Start	Finish	Resource Names
1	Talk with other project members.	0.5 days	5/19/2008	5/19/2008	Manager
2	Consider historical data.	0.5 days	5/19/2008	5/19/2008	Kris
3	Seek input from an expert.	0.5 days	5/20/2008	5/20/2008	Kris
4	Interview each person.	2.25 days	5/20/2008	5/22/2008	Barbara, Marcus, Laura
5	Interview IT support.	2 hrs	5/20/2008	5/20/2008	
6	Interview word processors.	2 hrs	5/20/2008	5/20/2008	
7	Interview report clerks.	2 hrs	5/21/2008	5/21/2008	
8	Interview mail processors.	2 hrs	5/21/2008	5/21/2008	
9	Interview payment clerks.	2 hrs	5/22/2008	5/22/2008	
10	Interview VP secretary.	2 hrs	5/22/2008	5/22/2008	
11	Gather examples for each function.	1.5 days	5/23/2008	5/26/2008	Carla
12	Gather resource information.	1.5 days	5/23/2008	5/26/2008	Carla
13	Hold Project team meeting.	0.5 hrs	5/26/2008	5/26/2008	All
14	Order materials.	1 hr	5/26/2008	5/26/2008	Carla
15	Type initial descriptons.	2 days	5/26/2008	5/28/2008	Renee, Elena
16	Edit.	1 day	5/28/2008	5/29/2008	Henri
17	Revise.	2 days	5/29/2008	6/2/2008	Renee, Elena
18	Versions 1: Document	0 days	6/2/2008	6/2/2008	Milestone
19	Meet with team again.	0.5 hrs	6/2/2008	6/2/2008	All
20	Meet with sensors, stakeholders.	1 hr	5/30/2008	6/2/2008	Manager, Sponsor
21	Revise.	2.5 days	6/3/2008	6/5/2008	Renee, Elena
22	Final proofread.	1.5 days	6/5/2008	6/6/2008	Henri
23	Copy document.	1 day	6/9/2008	6/9/2008	Arturo, Henri
24	Bind document.	0.5 days	6/10/2008	6/10/2008	Joe, Henri
25	Version 2: Document	0 days	6/10/2008	6/10/2008	Milestone
26	Controlled rollout.	0.5 days	6/11/2008	6/11/2008	All
27	Test the document.	2.5 days	6/11/2008	6/13/2008	All
28	Hold Project team meeting.	2 hrs	6/16/2008	6/16/2008	All
29	Costs, revisions, etc.	0 hrs	6/16/2008	6/16/2008	Milestone
30	Meet with Sponsor for OK.	2 hrs	6/17/2008	7/1/2008	Manager, Sponsor
31	Update the document.	3 days	7/1/2008	7/4/2008	Renee, Elena
32	Revise.	1 day	7/4/2008	7/7/2008	Manager
33	Type revised version.	1.5 days	7/7/2008	7/8/2008	Renee, Elena
34	Proofread.	0.5 days	7/8/2008	7/9/2008	Henri
35	Version 3: Document	0 days	7/9/2008	7/9/2008	Milestone
36	Copy document.	1 day	7/9/2008	7/10/2008	Arturo, Henri
37	Bind document.	1 day	7/10/2008	7/11/2008	Joe, Henri
38	Final distribution.	0.5 days	7/11/2008	7/11/2008	Joe, Arturo
39	Close Project.	0.5 days	7/11/2008	7/14/2008	Manager

Action 6: Create the Project Schedule and its Associated Gantt Chart

1.   Evaluate the schedule again with the team.

2. Review list of assumptions or constraints with the team.

3. Graph this information onto a Gantt chart, or similar one, to identify any areas where work is "crunching" up. Adjust for those times.

4. Update the network diagram to reflect the schedule dates.

CASE STUDY: BINH VO

When it comes to creating a project schedule, Binh Vo cautions new project managers not to believe the project plan is the project schedule. He gives this example:

"Suppose your sponsor tells you that he wants new software in the spring of 2009. New project managers might be tempted to believe that the schedule is "between now and spring of 2009." That is not your schedule.

"Furthermore, you should be sure to understand what your sponsor desires. Only then can you start to plan your project and put together a good schedule.

"For instance, does new software in 2009 mean that the software should be ready for anyone to go and install, or does it mean it is developed, running, and everyone in the organization has it? Ask questions — many questions — to be sure you have all the facets of what your sponsor is seeking."

A6:S1. Evaluate the schedule again with the team. Double check any days that a team member will not be available. It may seem odd that this step would be the first on this list when we just reviewed it during the last list.

There are some areas of project management when you will review things continuously as you work the project. The planning stages are when the most attention to detail is required. Therefore, you will go over items more than once; in this instance, you did the first pass by yourself. Now it is time to share your work with the team members and get their input.

Many seasoned project managers will do a final polling of the project team before publishing the schedule. A simple memo in e-mail requiring each member to respond by close of the business day, containing language similar to, "please advise me of any days off that you intend to take between start date and end date." You also want to gather the same information about your sponsor and key stakeholders because they likely will have meetings, conferences, or days out of the office, too. Your goal in the short term is to gather as much data as you can and then cover your second version in a team meeting and in the long term to produce a realistic schedule. You will want to account for all exceptions, such as lag time and lead time.

Lag time is the time delay between the start or finish of one activity and the start or finish of the next activity. For instance, if you are rehabbing a house, you will want to let the paint dry on the wall before you hang a picture. In that example, hanging a picture is linked to painting the wall — you do not want to hang the picture before you paint — however, you need to wait for the paint to dry. Therefore, you need to build in lag time of a reasonable interval for the paint to dry before you hang the picture. Figure 5-9 is a diagram of lag time.

Lead time is the overlap in time when the start of one activity occurs before the ending of another. This is also sometimes referred to as negative lag time. If a task can begin when its predecessor is half-finished, you can say that the lead time for the successor task is 50 percent.

To see how this works, let us use the rehabbing of a house as our example.

Say you have to paint the living room and dining room and the sum of those rooms equals the activity called paint. You allot two days for paint in your schedule. The next activity on the list, which is dependent on paint, is carpet. At the point when your painter completes the painting in the living room and moves all of his equipment into the dining room, do you wait to start on Activity carpet? Not if you are expedient. You will begin carpet in the living room while the painter is 50 percent done with the entire Activity paint. This is an example of a 50 percent lead time.

FIGURE 5-9: EXAMPLES OF LAG TIME AND LEAD TIME

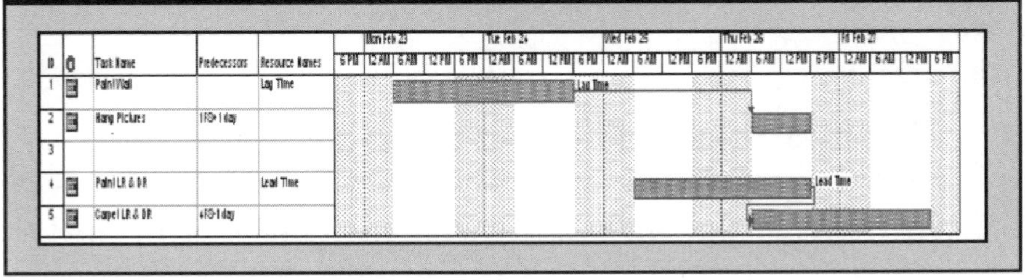

A6:S2. Review your list of assumptions or constraints. Similar to how you reevaluated your scheduling with your team, you will want to do the same exercise when comprising your list of assumptions or constraints. You want to demonstrate all the variables that govern the success of your outcome. You send a request out to your team and receive the following possible examples that you had not considered.

- We will produce the handbook in-house.

- We will not jeopardize the normal workday demands.

- We will use average-grade white copy paper.

- We will hole-punch and place the final deliverable in one-inch binders.

- We will copy double-sided.

- We will not incur overtime pay.

- We will not work weekends or evenings.

- We will not accept anything less than the level of quality that we would use when delivering a client document.

  ° There will be no hand-written corrections.

  ° There will be no smudges on the pages.

  ° There will be no typographical errors.

  ° We will use 12-point font and one-inch margins.

- Every copy will have an invitation to offer us feedback or corrections.

You need to think through your assumptions, because they will define your out-of-bound conditions. Say, for example, that the copy machine blows up and the mechanic who is scheduled to fix it cannot come for two days. What will happen to your project?

One of your assumptions was that you would copy it "in-house." Do you push the deliverable past your project end date, or do you look at outsourcing the copy function? Your assumptions also say that you will produce a certain level of quality. Therefore, your decision about how to resolve this issue is also governed by your quality assumption.

A6:S3. Graph this information onto a Gantt chart. The Gantt chart, sometimes called a bar chart, is a chart composed of bars on a schedule and other symbols to illustrate multiple, time-based activities or projects on a horizontal time scale. The chart in Figure 5-8, demonstrating lag and lead time, is a Gantt chart.

The one drawback to using standard Gantt charts is that the boxes do not show how one activity will affect another. There is no interconnection in standard Gantt charts. Today, software has updated the Gantt chart, and many applications feature interdependent links between bars. This type of Gantt chart is called a time line critical path schedule. The critical path is the sequence of activities in a project that take the longest time to complete, thereby determining the minimum schedule for a project.

A Gantt chart is also used to display project milestones — points in the project that mark the attainment of a goal or a set of tasks. In our example, the first draft of the deliverable is our first milestone. The Gantt chart depicts it with a black diamond on June 2.

The activity list that we comprised is graphed in a time line critical path Gantt chart, as shown in figure 5-10.

FIGURE 5-10: GANTT CHART: VERSION 1

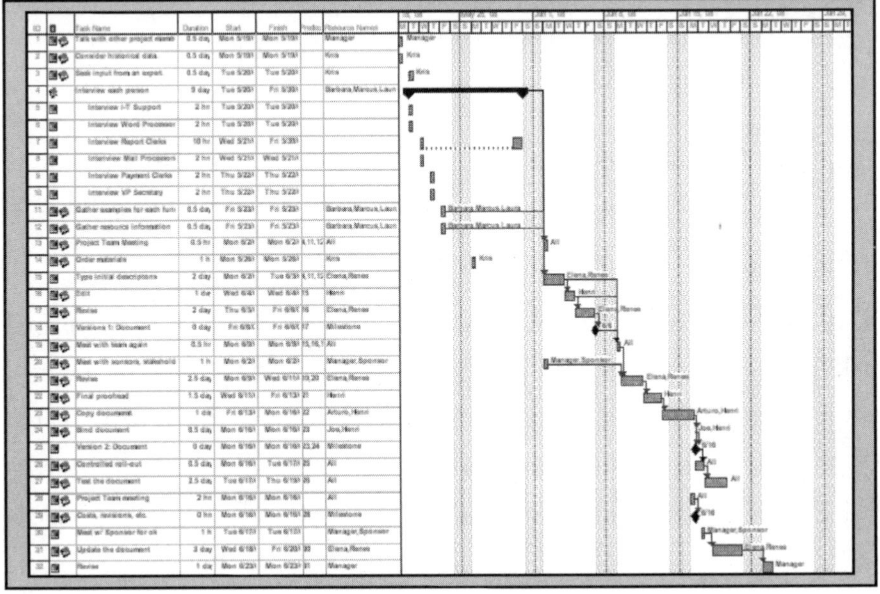

A6:S4. Update the network diagram to reflect the schedule dates.

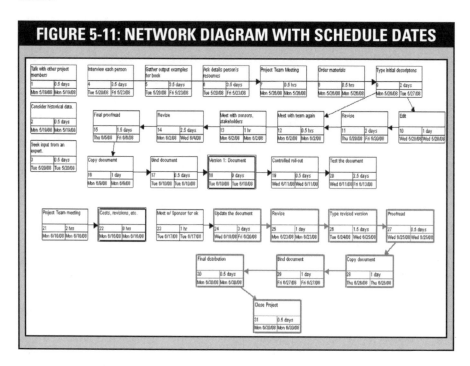

FIGURE 5-11: NETWORK DIAGRAM WITH SCHEDULE DATES

Action 7: Estimate the Costs

1. Obtain information about the rates or prices your resources will demand.

2. Create a worksheet showing each resource, the cost and duration of the resource, miscellaneous costs, and the sum.

A7:S1. Obtain information about the rates or prices your resources will demand. In our example, you are the manager of the people who are working on the project so you will already have their salary information. In the real world, you will find it more common that the project team consists of employees who do not report to you.

Therefore, you will need to obtain such data from their respective managers or the human resources department.

Once you have the information needed, you will calculate the cost of your resources for the time that you expect to need them. (See next step.)

A7:S2. Create a worksheet showing each resource and its associated cost and duration. As part of your effort, you may need to create assumptions and conditions that will create an out-of-bound condition such as "Materials not purchased in x grade will create a reduction in quality." You may also need to obtain your company's rules of hiring outside resources or buying materials.

There are two types of resources to consider: people and products.

People: Calculate the hourly rate for each employee as needed. Take that information and plug it into the software you are using, or calculate it manually. Microsoft Excel or a similar spreadsheet will easily tabulate your costs.

List each person in Column A, their hourly wage in Column B, and the number of hours you expect them to work the project in Column C. Multiply Column B by Column C and list the product in Column D.

Hint: The Gantt chart that you already loaded automatically summarizes the total person hours. As an alternative, you can sum it manually.

Regardless of whether you use Excel, the back of an envelope, or a project management software system, your output should extrapolate your costs in a format similar to the table here.

Upon summing the total costs per person and multiplying that by his or her hourly wage, you will quickly see where any disparity exists.

In the table below, the contrast between the 88 hours that Elena and Renee are carrying and their associated costs and the 20-hour average for the balance of the team is apparent. This is something you need to revisit, and we will discuss how to level off overallocated resources. Leveling is the process of shirting resources to even out the work load of team members and equipment, especially during times of peaks and valleys.

Products: You will want to assign any per-use rates for non-people resources such as a ream of paper, a box of toner, a set number of binders, postage and delivery costs, incentive costs — such as a pizza lunch for the team — and any other resource costs associated with your project. Your team will help you extrapolate these costs as you step through your meetings. You will enter these types of costs as fixed in your spreadsheet.

FIGURE 5-12: ESTIMATED COSTS BY RESOURCE

Resource	Group	Rate/Hr	Hrs Needed	Cost/Use	Overtime Rate
Manager	Management	$30.00	20.0	$600.00	$30.00
Barbara	VP Secretary	$18.00	18.0	$324.00	$27.00
Marcus	PayCenter	$10.00	18.0	$180.00	$15.00
Laura	Reports	$11.50	18.0	$207.00	$17.25
Arturo	MailRoom	$11.50	20.0	$230.00	$17.25
Joe	MailRoom	$9.50	16.0	$152.00	$14.25
Elena	Word Processing	$12.00	88.0	$1,056.00	$18.00
Renee	Word Processing	$12.00	88.0	$1,056.00	$18.00
Henri	Reports	$15.00	52.0	$780.00	$22.50
Kris	I-T support	$10.00	8.0	$80.00	$15.00
Daniel	Reports	$9.00	0.0	$0.00	$13.50
Carla	PayCenter	$12.50	25.0	$312.50	$18.75
Total Project Cost (Personnel)				$4,977.50	

Once you have completed the cost estimate for personnel, consider the other resources you will require. Before you can correctly enter costs, find out the costs that your company allocates for supplies.

Many firms have negotiated sale prices with office supply houses, which allows you to buy supplies at discounted rates. Asking about your company's methods and procedures to buy supplies may save your department money. Further, you will be ensuring that you follow your company's guidelines for ordering supplies. It is likely that your firm has established thresholds for how much each person can spend, by rank and/or by department.

As a new manager, the last thing you will want to do is run up a $3,000 supply charge, only to find out later that you are authorized only to approve $500 at your managerial level. Check first, and order later.

Once you have identified your parameters and processes, load the fixed costs you expect to incur into your planning spreadsheet. For our exercise, we assume we will need the following:

- Thirty pages of paper copied 250 times = 7,500 sheets of paper. Your company can buy 5,000 sheets of white paper for $30, and you will need two of those orders. Estimated costs for paper = $60

- Toner for the copy machine is $400 per cartridge, and one is all you will need to copy the number of pages for the project.

- You will require 250 one-inch binders at $3 each = $750

- Table of contents dividers at $1 for a set = $250

- Postage to mail binders to appropriate branches = $437.50

- Miscellaneous, such as incentive lunch, meeting beverages = $350

Now that you have loaded your variable and fixed costs, you have the beginning of what will become your budget. You load your data into a spreadsheet and total them, by activity, as shown in Figure 5-13.

FIGURE 5-13: INITIAL COST ESTIMATES FOR PROJECT

ID	Task Name	Fixed cost	Variance	Total Cost
1	Talk with other project members.	$0.00	$120.00	$120.00
2	Consider historical data.	$0.00	$40.00	$40.00
3	Seek input from an expert.	$0.00	$40.00	$40.00
4	Interview each person.	$0.00	$711.00	$711.00
4.1	Interview IT support.	$0.00	$0.00	$0.00
4.2	Interview word processors.	$0.00	$0.00	$0.00
4.3	Interview report clerks.	$0.00	$0.00	$0.00
4.4	Interview mail processors.	$0.00	$0.00	$0.00
4.5	Interview payment clerks.	$0.00	$0.00	$0.00
4.6	Interview VP secretary.	$0.00	$0.00	$0.00
5	Gather examples for each function.	$0.00	$150.00	$150.00
6	Gather resource information.	$0.00	$150.00	$150.00
7	Hold Project team meeting.	$0.00	$0.00	$0.00
8	Order materials.	$0.00	$2,347.50	$2,347.50
8.1	Paper	$60.00	$0.00	$60.00
8.2	Binders	$750.00	$0.00	$750.00
8.3	Toner	$400.00	$0.00	$400.00
8.4	Dividers	$250.00	$0.00	$250.00
8.5	Postage	$437.50	$0.00	$437.50
8.6	Misc ie Lunch, Sodas	$350.00	$0.00	$350.00
9	Type initial descriptons.	$0.00	$384.00	$384.00
10	Edit.	$0.00	$120.00	$120.00
11	Revise.	$0.00	$384.00	$384.00
12	Versions 1: Document	$0.00	$0.00	$0.00
13	Meet with team again.	$0.00	$0.00	$0.00
14	Meet with sonsors, stakeholders.	$0.00	$60.00	$60.00
15	Revise.	$0.00	$480.00	$480.00
16	Final proofread.	$0.00	$180.00	$180.00
17	Copy document.	$0.00	$212.00	$212.00
18	Bind document.	$0.00	$98.00	$98.00
19	Version 2: Document	$0.00	$0.00	$0.00
20	Controlled rollout.	$0.00	$0.00	$0.00
21	Test the document.	$0.00	$0.00	$0.00
22	Project Team meeting	$0.00	$0.00	$0.00
23	Costs, revisions, etc.	$0.00	$0.00	$0.00
24	Meet with Sponsor for OK.	$0.00	$60.00	$60.00
25	Update the document.	$0.00	$576.00	$576.00
26	Revise.	$0.00	$240.00	$240.00
27	Type revised version.	$0.00	$288.00	$288.00
28	Proofread.	$0.00	$60.00	$60.00
29	Version 3: Document	$0.00	$0.00	$0.00
30	Copy document.	$0.00	$212.00	$212.00
31	Bind document.	$0.00	$196.00	$196.00
32	Final distribution.	$0.00	$84.00	$84.00
33	Close Project.	$0.00	$120.00	$120.00
	TOTALS	$2,247.50	$7,312.50	$9,560.00

Clearing for Takeoff

I n this chapter, we will complete the activities in the planning phase that we began in Chapter 5. Specifically, we will cover the following actions:

8. Create a budget for each resource.

9. Create a variance plan.

10. Establish the quality constraints.

11. Create a communications plan.

12. Create a risk management plan.

13. Create the project plan, based upon all the above.

Phase II: Create the Project Plan (Part Two)

In the last chapter, we estimated the costs associated with each activity. Based upon the results of your initial costs, you are satisfied that your estimates appear to be under your budgeted cap of $10,000. However, as you scan the list, you notice some activities do not have any associated costs, such as team meetings. You will need to reevaluate and modify those data entry points when you do your leveling exercise. Before you start to tear apart your work, however, look at the choices of budgets and choose one.

Action 8: Create Your Project's Budget

1. Decide what kind of budget you will use.

2. Create a worksheet that integrates your cost sheet and activities to comprise a budget.

A1:S1. Decide what kind of budget you will use:

a. **Bottom-up estimating:** Estimate the cost of each individual activity and total them to obtain the entire cost of the project. This is the preferred method of budgeting, since it is considered the most accurate.

b. **Top-down estimating:** Use the actual costs from a previous and/or similar project to estimate the costs for the current project.

c. **Fixed-budget estimating:** Take the sum of the money you have been allocated and divide it across the project's activities to see what you cannot afford.

A8:S2. Create a worksheet that integrates your cost sheet and activities to comprise a budget.

Let us begin with a formula that you need to know.

$$\text{People} + \text{Resources} + \text{Time} = \text{Budget}$$

As a new manager, you might be tempted to focus more on pleasing your superiors than creating a realistic budget. Do not be tempted to give them an unrealistic number. In the end, they will prefer a realistic number that took longer to get to them over a fabulous number that was unrealistic. If they press you for a budget number before you have one ready, do not give them one. Rehearse this occurrence. Be prepared to say, "I do not yet have that number, and the last thing I would want to do is give you something that is unrealistic. We are working diligently at it, however." Giving them a message equivalent to your refusal to guess will gain their respect, ultimately — although perhaps not immediately.

There are two steps in deciding how to build a good budget. One is to pick the type of budget you will use. The other is to apply costs to each activity level.

A rule of thumb is that the more detail you can apply when building your budget, the more likely your accuracy will be. Although "ballpark estimates" are sometimes applicable, it is far better to use actual numbers whenever you can.

The use of actuals can be applied as either top-down estimating or bottom-up estimating.

In the top-down model, you would look to a former project that was done with comparable costs and apply those to your project. A wise project manager will apply precautionary measures to ensure that the costs are comparable before applying them to the current project.

For example, suppose you are working on a project for a local bakery that delivers cakes all over town. If this particular bakery catered a big event a year ago and it was time to plan for this year's gala, would it be practical to use the costs from last year? Perhaps, but the project manager should look at the cost of goods used, such as sugar, flour, frosting, and pans and compare them to this year.

Once that was evaluated, would the rest of the costs from last year apply? What about the cost of utilities? Is gas or electric heat the same price as a year ago? What about labor costs? What about the cost of fuel for transportation in the trucks? Would we want to apply fuel costs that were nearly a dollar cheaper per gallon to this year's transportation estimates? A "reality check" is always necessary when using a top-down approach.

The most accurate of all budget forecasting is the bottom-up approach, and we will use that for our model. In this instance, the project manager will apply the individual cost of each activity level and sum them up to obtain the budget required for the project.

Action 9: Create a Variance Plan

1. Define the conditions by which an unacceptable variance occurs.

2. Identify the root cause.

A9:S1. Define the conditions by which an unacceptable variance occurs. A variance occurs when an expected value of a condition differs from an actual value of a condition. In our example, if we expect our expenses will be under $10,000, but they end up being $12,000, we have a $2,000 variance. In the world of project management, this large of a variance would be disastrous — if it came as a surprise.

We will discuss the importance of control in Chapter 8, but you will need to have a plan in place to identify when a variance is large enough to call it a variance that is creating an out-of-bound condition.

A9:S2. Identify the root cause. When you encounter a variance in your project, it is sometimes difficult to identify the cause. It may be that your time estimate of a particular activity was wrong or that the person doing the activity took too long. The most accurate means to find the cause is to compare it to a similar activity, if this information is available. Meet with your team to gather information and evaluate the data you have to date to determine whether there are any other variances. You will compare all the key elements of your baseline, such as:

1. **Schedule:** Compare the planned start and end date of each activity against the actual dates.

2. **Costs:** You will compare estimated personnel costs for all activities against actual hours worked and booked.

3. **Quality:** Compare the baseline estimate of how good the deliverable will be against what is currently being predicted.

By doing this exercise, you will flush out any additional variances or patterns that may help you assess the cause. If all the variances are occurring in the IT department, you will know there is an issue there and work to resolve it. You may discover that a large shipment of computers came back and the IT support had to reload all the office software that the sales persons need onto each machine – and that this requirement happened in the middle of the project activity dates.

If you discover nothing, you might have to assume this was an isolated occurrence, and you will need to plan for its impact to the entire project. You will want to watch to ensure it does not reoccur.

Two members of our panel of project managers reported how they handle variances. The first stressed ways to avoid them, and the second described the way they were dealt with.

CASE STUDY: PAUL SCHOEN

"Variances all go back to how well you time and cost estimate. That, in turn, goes back to how well you understood your deliverable. In my world, it depends on whether you are purchasing a product or producing one.

"Let us say you have to develop something — it is a time issue. You have to build the time estimate into your people, such as, 'I need a business analyst for six months; we do not have one in-house, so I will need to pay $90 an hour to contract one.' In this instance, you have to have your deliverables defined clearly first. Then ask again, what do you expect the deliverable to look like? You may encounter a conversation such as this, 'Well, I expected a big report.' 'Oh, I thought it would be smaller.' 'No, 100 pages because I want to include blah blah blah.' 'Oh, we did not have that built in.' It is very important to do this to help reduce your chances of encountering variances.

"I handle variances just as they come. If your boss tells you that you cannot have any because legislature says August 1, then you need to build buffers in to get it done. Recognize early if you are not going to make it, and go to your boss. State your problem as an opportunity. Make recommendations such as, 'We need to get more staff; it will cost a little money, but we will have more people trained.' Problems can be opportunities for new things."

CASE STUDY: MIKE HEUTMAKER

"Variances are handled case by case. If they are too large, we may cancel the project. If they are addressable, there is usually a negotiation between product management (the team that defined what was to be built) and engineering (the team that says how it will be built) to determine whether anything can be removed from the design to bring it back into the targeted product cost."

Action 10: Establish the Quality Constraints

1. Gather your quality policy, Scope Statement, deliverable specifications, and other data that govern the quality your company/sponsor expects.

2. Define what constitutes quality for each item.

3. Define quality measurements and controls.

Build in quality gateways to be included at several stages in the project. You will not want to close out any of the processes without a quality check.

You will use your measurements of cost and schedule as part of your quality statements.

A10:S1. Gather your quality policy, Scope Statement, deliverable specifications, and other data that govern the quality your company/sponsor expects. Every company is different. Some of the larger corporations will have quality managers in place with whom you can meet to ensure your quality standards are being met. A more common environment is one where you, as project manager, will need to learn a little about quality management.

Let us go over some basic terms.

Quality refers to the traits of each project's deliverable. These traits are predefined to meet the sponsor's and the stakeholders' requirements.

Quality assurance refers to the means to test the deliverables and their individual components before and during delivery to ensure the sponsor's specifications are met. You might hear about software quality assurance (SQA), especially if you work in an industry where software is being developed.

Quality control refers to an ongoing quality management and review of the process of doing the work of the project.

Quality management refers to the process required to ensure that a project will satisfy the needs for which it was deployed. Similar to project management, the person or people who run quality management are responsible for the quality of every process or product in an organization.

The quality management plan is the document that identifies the quality standards specific to the project and the means to satisfy them.

A10:S2. Define what constitutes quality for each item. As project manager, you will use your final deliverable to meet the standards of quality. Along the way, you will evaluate your measurements of cost and schedule as part of your quality statements. Each team member's performance may have a quality criteria set against it. Ultimately, it is up to you, your sponsor, and your key stakeholders to determine where quality is most important and exactly what are the standards that will be adhered to.

In our example, we may define our final deliverable to be of quality if it is easily read, copied without smudges, placed neatly into binders without any holes being torn, and the like.

A10:S3. Define quality measurements and controls. To ensure that all your quality standards are met, assuming you do not have a quality manager available to assist you, always have your quality attributes foremost in your mind. Perhaps this is something that is part of every meeting minutes. It can be displayed on the white board of your meeting room or typed, copied, and posted at the station of each team member. Do whatever it takes for everyone to understand the quality measurements that you are seeking.

Action 11: Create a Communications Plan

Communications technology is one of the fastest-changing industries in the world. There are now more ways to communicate with each other than ever before, and with that, there are more ways than ever to misunderstand each other.

As project manager, you will need to think through how you will communicate, with whom, how often, and using what medium. You will need to be in the loop of all information processing, from the most casual to the most formal.

CASE STUDY: PEGGY SANCHEZ

Peggy Sanchez has been a project manager at Digi International out of Minneapolis for about a year. She lists communication high on her list of things to master for optimum success.

She comments, "Keep communication constantly updated. Not only for the fairness of all the people committed, but also to cover yourself. Because occasionally, you will get the team member who spends more time thinking about how not to do things than to just get the task list done. Or, they come to meetings with attitudes and you hear, 'That is not my job,' or 'No one told me.' By having a central message board that is constantly updated, you can put the onus back on them.

"At our company, we use a couple of different ways to communicate the status. With Operations, everything has to be in writing. They use a Web program called TWiki™ that is like a bulletin board. It allows them to arrange things by project, post who is on the team, the schedule, the action item, part numbers, specs, and more.

"For schedules, we use Microsoft Project. It is relatively new to me, as PM, and so far, I am loving it. Before Project, we used action logs that were outdated the minute we concluded the meetings. Now, I just bring the schedule to the meeting and everybody updates things right there. More people are accountable. They also can see the precedents and decedents and no longer have to guess what has to come first. It saves a considerable amount of time.

CASE STUDY: PEGGY SANCHEZ

"This kind of communication brings accountability and eliminates some of the politics of having to 'report' about what other people have not done. It is a great communication tool."

Peggy's comments emphasize the importance of having a variety of communication methods for different venues. Consider the various types of communications: memos, e-mail, letters, reports, meetings, presentations, teleconferences, videoconferences (including Internet "Web conferences"), and telephone. You will need to know when to use each of these and what the rules are as you use them.

1. Gather organization information about all stakeholders, such as their titles, location, and phone numbers.

2. Understand corporate policy information about communication requirements and available technology to use for the project.

3. Obtain a statement from your sponsor describing his or her expectations and parameters about external communications (such as a press release).

4. Consider the variables of your communication needs. Include how information will be gathered, how it will be disseminated, by what type of medium, by whom, and how often.

5. Put together your communications plan.

A11:S1. Gather information about each stakeholder. The first thing to do is to assemble basic information about the people with whom you will be working. This list should include your sponsor(s), stakeholders, and all the members of your team. It may also include any other managers whom you will need to frequently contact. Create a spreadsheet listing each person's name, title, office location, e-mail address, and phone numbers. (**Note:** If your list contains any personal information, such as home address or phone numbers, be careful to ensure it is not shared inappropriately.)

A11:S2. Understand your corporate policy about communication requirements and available technology. Visit your human resources manager to obtain your company's rules about communications. You will want to know which limitations are in place for each type of method or technology. For instance, your company may restrict international calls or have a budget for the number of video conferences you can conduct, or it may require that any meetings scheduled in an executive conference room be approved by a certain level of management.

A11:S3. Obtain a statement from your sponsor describing his or her expectations and parameters about external communications. This step might be assumed if your project is strictly internal in its results. Throughout this book, we have been using the employee handbook as our simulated project. It is unlikely that your sponsor would want any kind of announcement to be made to the press about its release. Compare that to a sponsor's decision over a big release of a new version of Apple's iPod. Obviously, that sponsor would want to have several, staggered press releases to unveil a product of that magnitude.

Still, in our model, you might want to ask your sponsor for his thoughts about announcing the final deliverable to the other three regions in the company. Recall that you support the Central Region sales vice president and that there are three others with identical sales structures. Any time you can further your manager's successes outside his "home" area, you will make points for your manager and yourself.

A11:S4. Consider the variables of your communication needs. Include how information will be gathered and disseminated and how often it will be updated. Now that you have compiled your company's parameters, your sponsor's expectations, and your own perspective about the levels of communication required for your project, you are ready to draft a communications plan. You begin to group your objectives:

1. You will want to convey status about things, such as:

- Meetings

- Issues

- Deliverables conditions

- Documents

2. You will want to relate issues and needs with people, such as:

- Sponsors and executive sponsors

- Stakeholders

- Team members

  ° Include minimum expectations for deliverables review.

  ° Identify how the team will involve outside vendors (engage and track).

- Outside vendors

- Outside partners

- Other resources

3. You have an obligation to the project itself, such as:

- Status of scope, costs, and schedule

- Quality assurance

- Interval best used for communicating status

- Mechanisms best used for communicating status

4. You have an obligation to lead by example, in informal settings.

- Consider the amount of information disseminated informally. You are the project leader and people will notice:

  ° The words you use in your e-mails

  ° The way you communicate, verbally

  ° The way you use voice mail

If you have difficulty seeing the big picture, take a step back and ask, "Who needs to receive what information and how often?" This reality check will keep you focused where you need to be.

A11:S5. Apply the learning you acquired from Steps 1-4 and put together your communications plan. Our project's communication plan is found below.

THE PROJECT COMMUNICATION PLAN

Project Name: SUPPORT STAFF EMPLOYEE HANDBOOK

1. Stakeholders

This project has 22 stakeholders, consisting of the following groups:

- Sponsor (1)

- Project manager (1)

- Project team members (12)

- Regional representatives (5)

THE PROJECT COMMUNICATION PLAN

- Sales managers (3)

Extended team members consist of outside vendors who directly or indirectly benefit from the project's deliverable. Examples of this group include ABC Trophy Company that has, for the past three quarters, had to expedite our delivery of awards because we did not get our orders in promptly.

2. Communication Resources

- **TWiki™.** We expect to use a collaboration space at **www.twiki.org** where we will enter our status, next steps, and process parts at the end of each day. The purpose of using this Web site will be to showcase the project's process for all stakeholders to see at any time they choose. This type of public display is intended to communicate our status and to show who is next "up to bat." It is a method of removing any politics from the equation.

- **Microsoft Project.** We will also use Microsoft Project to manage the entire process, end to end. Whereas the information provided on **twiki.org** is provided at a summary level, the data loaded in Microsoft Project is dynamic and will show our status, up to the minute, for any team member to review.

- **E-mail.** The project manager will create and maintain a broadcast list containing the addresses of core team members and others, on an as-needed basis, to receive information of a noncritical nature that affects the entire team.

- **Teleconferencing/Videoconferencing.** The team will use teleconferencing only when it is necessary to include people in remote areas. The general expectation is that teleconferencing will not be required since all team members are located on site.

3. Formal Communications

- **Weekly Status Reports.** Each project team member will prepare a one-to two-page summary document in Microsoft Word and submit it to the project manager each Friday via Microsoft Outlook e-mail. The document will outline the progress accomplished, issues where a person requires assistance, and any recommendations or further comments. The report will conclude with a bulleted itemization of what the team member expects to accomplish in the coming week and each activity's associated, required resources.

THE PROJECT COMMUNICATION PLAN

- **Monday Team Meetings.** The project manager will address the issues from the team members' memos every Monday in the team meetings.

  The project manager will publish a formal agenda every week to each core team member who is expected to attend. The agenda will include the project manager's expected list of who needs to bring what to the meeting.

- **Meeting minutes.** An appointed team member will take notes and disseminate minutes to the project team via e-mail. This memo will clearly indicate who has an action item, what the item entails, and the due date for the activity.

- **Weekly updates.** The project manager will publish a Microsoft Word document identifying the updated plan requirements and status for the team.

4. Informal Communication

This is defined as faxes, phone calls, e-mails, and impromptu "water cooler" office discussions.

- Each team member commits to checking the fax machine, U.S. mail, and internal mail at least once daily.

- Each team member commits to checking voice mail and e-mail at least every other hour.

Action 12: Create a Risk Management Plan

1. Determine potential sources of risk by evaluating all your work thus far. Do any of the deliverables need to be produced for the first time? Is there any task not identified on the Work Breakdown Structure? Is there anyone on the staffing plan who might leave?

2. Quantify the impact that each risk would have, if incurred.

3. Mitigate risks. Take advance action to reduce the effect of risk and put together a contingency plan.

4. Create a risk management plan.

A12:S1. Determine potential sources of risk by evaluating all your work. A key component to the success of a project is to understand what risks will affect the project's intended outcome. A robust project will have well-defined expectations, cost justifications, and thorough resource allocation. However, many project managers are reluctant to even bring up risks, let alone prepare for them. There seems to be an underlying fear that simply by mentioning a potential risk the project might be in jeopardy. Yet, sponsors and stakeholders expect to know about any potential risk, so you, as project manager, have the task of identifying them and presenting them in a well-balanced presentation of the potential risks and your recommendations for their respective solutions.

Your first step is to evaluate your project's deliverable and decide which, if any, of the following statements are true:

a. The deliverable is not a core competency for our business.

b. The deliverable has never been done before.

c. The deliverable involves using untested technology.

If one of the statements is true, then obviously the risk is lower than if all three were true. In our simulation, statements one and two are true. Creating a handbook is not a core competency, and the handbook has not been done before. However, statement three is not true because we use the technology to create a handbook in our day-to-day duties. We can conclude that we are doing something outside our normal operations and it has never been done before: the risk factor for the deliverable is medium-high.

You then evaluate your Scope Statement. Are your costs and goals realistic? What about your resources? Is there any danger of anyone on the team leaving during the project?

A12:S2. Quantify the impact that each risk would have, if incurred. When quantifying the impact of each risk, consider the monetary, quality, and schedule impact. For example, suppose that Barbara (the vice-president's secretary) quits in the middle of the project. While this is unlikely to occur, the impact would be significant, because no one is cross-trained in her work. What might you do to prepare for that event, and what would be the impact to the project?

Obviously, since she will not be there to describe her duties, you will need to find someone else who can. This will require more time as you phone around the country to speak with other secretaries in other regions or hunt down the person who had the job before her. The other impact will be that she will not be in place to do her part of the project. What did you have her scheduled to do? Who will do that? Will you need to hire someone from a temporary agency to fill in? What will be the impact to cost?

Take a hard look at the work allocation table that you created in Chapter 5. Who has the most work assigned or carries responsibility along the critical path? Ask yourself what might happen if they left, also.

Identify the risks that would be the most devastating to your project.

A12:S3. Mitigate Risks. Take advance action to reduce the effect of risk and put together a contingency plan. When planning to mitigate risks, first evaluate whether you can eliminate them. For instance, if there is a big impact to the project if Barbara quits, you might consider asking her to write her job description early, before that stage in the project, or perhaps you will extend your schedule another week to allow for possible risks that may arise.

If you cannot eliminate each risk entirely, put together your thoughts for how you will mitigate them, if they arise. Create a contingency plan in advance, such as locating the person who held the position before Barbara and having that information ready. Call temporary agencies to inquire after their rates if you will need to hire someone, then change your budget to include this potential cost.

A12:S4. Create a risk management plan. Organize the information you evaluated in steps one through three into a document that describes the risks and their associated impact. Outline your contingency plan and recommendations and present them to your sponsor or key stakeholders.

Action 13: Create the Project Plan

A13. Pull it all together. Your project plan is almost comprised at this point. By stepping through each individual process, you have created your project plan in pieces. All you need to do now is have the team meeting as described in the Close Phase (below). You need to know that by creating your project plan, you have also created your baseline of measurements that will guide you through the rest of your project. A baseline is the plan that guides your costs, schedule, quality measurements, and other processes. It is called a baseline, or sometimes a baseline project plan, because this is the plan by which you will measure all your variances.

Close Phase II

Now you will close down the planning phase. You will want to have a formal meeting with your sponsor and stakeholders to discuss the project plan. If you have not provided them with your latest version of your plan yet, do so.

Request or arrange a meeting, depending on your corporate culture. During the meeting, be sure to review all sections of the plan. Newer project managers may be uncomfortable drawing attention to the pieces of the plan that are challenging. Do not shy away from it. Use those items as an opportunity to show your sponsor that you are concerned that the deliverable is of the highest quality. Stress to him or her why you are concerned about various parts and what you recommend. Your sponsor will appreciate having your well-considered recommendations about problem areas as part of your delivery.

The goal of this meeting is to ensure everyone is completely comfortable with the plan in its current version. If not, plans need to be outlined for required adaptations. You and your team will adjourn this meeting and go back to make the changes you discussed. Then, you will come back together to share the results of your changes to find out if you can proceed to the next phase.

When you reach a consensus, you will provide your sponsor with a sign-off sheet that documents that he or she is satisfied with the entire project. By approving your project plan, they have given you permission to begin your project.

Chapter 7

Takeoff

You should congratulate yourself at this point. You have taken your project from idea stage, assessed its feasibility, planned every aspect of its deployment, evaluated the possible risks, and comprised contingency plans, and you are finally ready to start your deliverable.

Many project managers claim this is the downhill part of the project. Having done excessive planning, your activity in this phase and the next one is merely following the steps for which you have planned so carefully. You will find that as project manager, your activity will be heavily involved with meetings and following up on meeting items.

As you step through the phase, your focus will be on ensuring the project is deployed within the constraints you set forth. You also will spend much time communicating to the team and the sponsors about your progress. A good project manager and team will keep an eye on detail to identify any variances. Should they occur, the team will resolve what it can and escalate what it cannot as quickly as these instances arise.

Phase III: Create a Draft of the Deliverables

Initiate Phase III

By now, you should be comfortable with the notion that everything in project management is done as a predefined process. Just as you close down one phase, you get buyoff from key personnel; the same applies to every phase that you open.

As you meet with your sponsor and key stakeholders to close out Phase II, you will also obtain permission to begin Phase III. As part of it, you will review the project plan, its deliverables, expected cost both with and without contingencies, the resources you will use, and the expected length of time it will require.

Note that we are working to create a draft of our deliverable in this phase. The term draft works well with the type of deliverable we are making. Be aware that this phase is primarily designed to fine-tune the specifications for the final deliverable, whatever it may be. In project management, you will often hear this phase associated with the concept of creating models. A model is a type of an example of reality, normally simplified for understanding the context. For our purposes, we will refer to our model as the draft.

Plan Phase III

Throughout the project, we have explored various means to communicate with your team and others. It bears discussion to address the importance of meetings, especially at this stage in the project. You and your team will now be executing your deliverables and then controlling their deployment. Your team members will be working the activities of the project. It is important to recognize that their time is already shortened to work on the project, and they may feel pressure with this added to their normal daily tasks.

Meaningful Progress Meetings

Over the next few pages, we will address some basics about meetings, then we will provide a checklist of things that will help you attain meaningful progress meetings. Finally, we will share insights from actual project managers about how they make meetings as effective as possible.

As a new manager, you can be assured that you will be tested on many levels. One level is how you conduct meetings. There are all sorts of ways you will be challenged, normally by people disrupting the meeting, trying to take control away from you, or using the platform for their own personal agenda. No matter what your meeting topic, it is universally true that you never want to have a meeting for the sake of a meeting. There is an agenda with an expectation of accomplishing something, such as decisions, education, resolution, or planning.

Throughout the disruptions, you need to demonstrate control. If you can do this amicably, with a level of finesse, it will not hurt you. As a new manager, you do not want to come with a gavel and start banging the table for order — not just yet, anyway.

So, how might you handle the following situations?

Cell phones. Always announce that cell phones should be turned off or put on vibrate at the onset of the meeting. For the first few times you lead a meeting, you might want to stress the importance of this by asking, "Do I have everyone's agreement that cell phones will be off for the next 15 (or 30) minutes?" Get team buy-in.

Sidebar conversations. When two or three people start whispering or having a private conversation, it is aggravating to the others in the room. Of course, most meetings have brief exchanges between members that are nondisruptive such asking one's neighbor what was just said. However, when people's sidebar conversations become that — conversations — you need to stop it as soon as possible. Normally, a simple comment such as "One conversation here, please," will be enough. However, for persistent chatterers, you may need to call attention to them directly. Do it with respect, with a comment such as, "Marcus and Joe, is your discussion something that would be helpful to our overall topic, here?" They may surprise you and say that it is. In which case, invite them to discuss it. Depending on what it is, you can either discuss it as a group or ask them to hold it for a later time. Your goal is to get through your meeting's agenda.

Latecomers. People who arrive late not only disrupt the entire meeting, but they cause rework because they require others to fill them in. Do not fill them in during the meeting. Continue as if they had been there all along. Let them find out what they missed later, or you are penalizing everyone who arrived on time. You may find this particularly difficult if the person who arrives late is a sponsor or a big wheel. But stick to your guns, unless the person expressly asks you about a specific element of what he or she missed.

Coughers. It may be unavoidable, but the person who is persistently coughing during a meeting drowns out much of the discussion. Many team leaders will have a bowl of candy on the desk for a couple of reasons. One is for morale and the other is in case someone has need to moisten a dry throat, for whatever reason. If you choose this route, you should include some sugar-free choices in the mix, also. If there is water or candy in the room available, you will want to invite the cougher to take care of it, politely. You may say something like, "Would you like to step out in the hallway and get something for that?" If he or she does so, great; if not, and the coughing continues, make your next comment a statement rather than a question. "Please, go outside and get something for that cough." The others will thank you for it.

Interrupters. This is one of the rudest behavioral traits a person can display, whether in a meeting or outside one. You want to be polite but firm and simply say, "Please, let Barbara finish, then we will hear from you."

Orators. There are those people who need to have the spotlight upon them, at any opportunity. They disrupt meetings by taking the conversation off to a tangent about something nonrelated — and usually to do with them — or they ramble endlessly as they make their point. During these types of scenarios, you have to be the one to interrupt, but do so with a smile and say, politely, "How does this situation fit into what we are discussing now?" Track them back on the course. If the point they are making is a valid one and should be considered but it was not on your agenda, either agree to include it in the next meeting or address it outside the meeting.

Arguers. A discussion is considered to be a meaningful exchange of ideas, while an argument is a stalemate where one or more parties continually states his or her position and refuses to yield to other possibilities. If you come across an argument, recognize it immediately and pull the team back on the track. "People, we have strong opinions here, but what do we need in order to come to a decision about our issue?" Steer them toward identifying the various components required to make the decision, or proceed with the plan. Should you encounter a situation where people will not budge on a certain point, try what professional negotiators do: use the set-aside method. "All right, I see how we are going to be stuck on the issue of how we distribute our handbook to the other regions, so let us put that issue aside for now. Let us move to the issue of which binders to use." Finish as much as possible, then come back to the set-asides. A series of agreements might be enough to break the stalemate. If not, you might need to take a vote or add it to your issues list for later resolution. In the worst-case scenario, you might consider escalating it. We will address that process later.

Attackers. One of the hardest issues to deal with in a meeting is a team member who is so rude as to make attacking or belligerent remarks to another, even to you. There are three common circumstances when this behavior will arise. First, if the person is extremely frustrated and unaware of how his or her words are being perceived. Second, if the person feels somehow protected in his or her job and has no fear of crossing a line. Finally, if the person is so beyond able to cope with the pressures of his or her job that being fired is preferable to remaining employed. Should you encounter this situation, assume that he or she is unaware and offer a graceful escape to the effect of, "I am sure you do not mean to say that, really. We are all frustrated here. Let us all calm down."

If you have any lingering issues with personnel that need to be addressed, follow up with it in the privacy of your office, one on one. Some people are not testing you but are truly in need of performance reviews for their behavior. However, if you handle these types of situations objectively and quickly, you will achieve the greatest success in finishing your meeting on time with your agenda points covered.

Now that we have covered how to handle disruptions, let us look at the other items that you should consider when striving for a meaningful progress meeting.

Determine the Need for a Meeting

- Determine whether the meeting is even required or if you can accomplish the same thing by telephone, e-mail, or a similar device.

- Ensure there is something new to discuss and that you are not having this meeting just because one is scheduled.

Effective Preparation

- Determine the meeting's purpose.

- Define the sequence of work you expect to get done.

Consider:

- ° What needs to happen at this meeting?

- ° What are my expected dates for each outcome to happen?

- ° Which person is going to be responsible for each outcome?

- ° What does he or she need?

- Review any open items before the meeting so that you have a status for anything you were to address to the group. Consider:

  - ° What has happened before this meeting?

  - ° What questions or issues are still outstanding? Who is responsible for these responses?

- Prepare the agenda.

- Decide how long the meeting needs to be — a general rule is no more than 15 or 30 minutes.

- Invite the right people, such as team members to weekly meetings and shareholders to key milestone meetings.

- Advise people what they need to prepare for the meeting, if anything.

- Consider which tools you will use during the meeting and request any materials, as appropriate.

  - ° Brainstorming — White board

    °   Flip charts — Easel and paper

    °   Microsoft scheduling — Audio-visual equipment

Begin on Time

- Begin even if some people have not yet arrived.

- Say the purpose of the meeting, the duration, and any background items, if required.

- Request all cell phones to be turned off.

- Assign someone to keep time so you know the half time of the meeting, five minutes before conclusion, and conclusion.

- Assign someone to take minutes, if this function is not already assigned.

- Say the goal of the meeting.

- Review any background items or minutes, if necessary.

Lead the Team to Participation

- Encourage members to participate as evenly as possible; do not let one or two monopolize the discussion.

- Control the discussion so that things are moving forward and you stick to the agenda.

- Consistently seek team understanding and commitment.

- Understand each outcome you are seeking and who is responsible for what before you conclude the meeting.

Close the Meeting

- If time is up, close the meeting; likewise, if you are finished but time still remains, close the meeting.

- Summarize your accomplishments or recommendations.

- Advise who will be publishing the follow-up items and minutes and by what time, later that day.

Tips on Meetings from the Project Managers

Following is a compilation of comments from some project managers about how they communicate or use meetings.

CASE STUDY: PEGGY SANCHEZ

Peggy Sanchez was delighted to find a time-saving use for Microsoft Project in her progress meetings:

"Microsoft Project is used for the schedules in our company. I found out by bringing it directly to the progress meeting that we can all work it in real time. I pull up the schedule of activities, and everybody looks at it instead of action logs.

"Then, we update things right there in the meeting. I can go right down the list and ask after what has been done. More people are accountable because they see their task there and they know it is up to them to keep their piece going. Plus, you can see the precedents. This reduces a lot of time because we do not have to keep updating the schedule all the time. Before, as soon as we posted it, it was out of date. Instead, we bring it to the meeting and add tasks, adjust dates, break down tasks — whatever we need to do.

"This activity also has the benefit of eliminating some of the politics of having to report about what other people might not have accomplished. They see it, real time, right in the meeting, and can explain what happened. For instance, if they needed to get something from someone else and that person was out, we talk about how else to get the information or whether we need to adjust the schedule. It becomes more of a team effort than a shame and blame thing."

CASE STUDY: PAUL SCHOEN

Paul Schoen uses a combination of progress meetings mixed with e-mail communications to keep people up to date:

"If we are working a big project, we have weekly meetings and utilize white boards. We use the master schedule to keep us on track. One of the most important skills of an effective project manager is to utilize communication well.

"I make sure that our meeting notes come out the same day while they are fresh and people can adjust them right away if clarification is needed. Then, I use e-mail as a means to communicate during the week, between meetings.

"E-mail helps a lot. You do not have to have a meeting to get things accomplished. Send an e-mail, pick up the phone, or if you really need something, go straight to that person's office and stay there until you get it. Do not be afraid to go to your boss's boss if he is your sponsor."

CASE STUDY: DAN MASON

Dan Mason describes how he found his own way to best communicate and conduct meetings, after taking over the job from someone else:

"Well, when I was following the lead of the former project manager, she did it better than me. I worked on a project team for ten years before I was promoted, almost two years ago, so I thought it would be easy. But when it was my turn to do it, I found it was taking me too long to do everything she did.

"She had status reports coming in e-mail, quickie items in text messages to my cell phone, and then there was the whole Monday morning report thing where we had to prepare a blow-by-blow report of our progress and bring it to the meeting. It eats up too much time to report about how you are doing to that extent, at least when I try to do it.

"Today, I use e-mail to keep people on track. I log activity in Microsoft Project and disseminate it accordingly. I schedule our team for Monday morning meetings, but that is where I differ from my predecessor. I do not come to the

CASE STUDY: DAN MASON

meeting expecting how each person is going to perform. I come there to talk about activities with them and let them tell me how each one is going and where they need help. Then, if they do not step up to the tasks we need done, or if I feel someone who has volunteered is better matched elsewhere, I will move people around. I do not see myself as the director — more like the editor. My team drives a lot of what goes on. I just keep everyone else on track, mostly through Microsoft products like Project, Excel, and Outlook for e-mail."

CASE STUDY: CHRISTINA MAJEED

Christina Majeed relies heavily on meetings to communicate and keep her team moving forward, as she describes, below:

"We communicate by telephone. We have many conference calls, and we send e-mails to groups specific to the project. We use Excel for much of our work and share our sheets via e-mail. Plus, we use an internal database where we can go to figure out what we need for the clients.

"We use the software that we sell to our clients. On our network, people can log in and see up to the minute. At our company, we have morning meetings every day. During that meeting, we set the tone for the whole day and review what was accomplished the day before.

"I always do plenty of planning for a meeting. If I do not get it done on Sunday evening, I get to work early on Monday. I look at what happened last week, what was accomplished, and evaluate what I want to accomplish this week. I map it out carefully. Then we use the daily meetings to communicate about how we are doing and where we need help. Running meetings very efficiently is key. It is important to keep people focused on the agenda, go through each topic, and come away with a plan. Our meetings are never longer than 15-30 minutes."

CASE STUDY: BOB ECKERT

Bob Eckert discusses how he runs multiple projects with resources across several geographic areas:

"I am managing five projects right now, which is typical. At our company, one person is assigned to a large project, which by our standards, is more than a year in length. Smaller projects can be grouped into a portfolio for another manager to run. That is my situation, at present.

"I have remote resources and whenever you run a project with remote resources – it increases the complexity. Communication is a bit more difficult. That face-to-face discussion buys a lot. What you may be saying on the phone may not be perceived. They can't look at the white board or see your expression. So, we are starting to use more web-based meeting platforms but it's too soon to report how effective they are, for us. So you can see how it's critical that I keep everyone aligned while we migrate over.

"A long time ago, a friend told me whenever you are talking about project issues, direct the team to the project schedule. It makes it less personal and focuses them on what needs to be done. At our progress meetings, we review the schedule with them and say, 'We made an agreement that this date is what we are shooting for. How can we make this date if ___?' Or, 'This task has your name next to it so you need to tell me, how can we get it done?' If they say they need help from so and so, we bring so and so in, to help.

"I also rely on the issues list that I created. This is a simple Excel spreadsheet. It has an issue number, a high-level description, date it was created, what the detail is, when the issue was resolved, and what the resolution was. We review that at our progress meetings, too."

Mr. Eckert was kind enough to provide an example of the issues list that he tracks and updates during his meetings. It is provided below.

No.	Description of Issue	Date Opened	Person Responsible	Description of Impact to the Project	Priority	Status	Date Resolved	Description of Resolution	Issue Initiator
1	What is the issue?	12/29/2007	Bob Eckert	How does this issue affect the project?	Low, Medium or High?	Open or Closed?		What is the resolution?	Who initiated the issue?
2									
3									
4									
5									

CASE STUDY: SARY MABJISH

Sary Mabjish relies on meeting minutes. From the minutes, his team creates a list of action items, which is then published. He explains how this works well:

"In every meeting, we take meeting minutes and detail the action items that are completed and ones still pending. We then publish the minutes so that everyone is on the same page. This saves time in the end because people are not saying, 'No, that is not what we agreed upon.' They have a chance to clarify it right away.

"Publishing action items with due dates beside the person responsible is crucial for the project to succeed, and in every meeting, we follow up on the action items from the previous meeting. If something is complete, it is marked completed and stays there — not erased. The ones that are pending, we keep working toward the due date or reassign the due date, if something needs to be adjusted.

"This is particularly important when you are working on six or seven projects at the same time. You still have to work on all the details and schedules for each. This is where your skills come into effect. Pay attention to the action items — use the documents with the schedule. I rely on that heavily. I review it before I go to each meeting and follow up as needed. The worst you can do is walk in to a meeting unprepared, and they will be asking questions, not knowing what happened. You are the person who is motivating and pushing them, and if you are not ready, they will not be in a mind-set to accomplish anything."

Execute & Control Phase III

Now that we have covered the way to achieve a meaningful meeting and to communicate with people during and between your meetings, you are ready to begin them. The purpose of your meetings during this phase will be to monitor progress. In particular, you will be concerned with the following:

- Evaluate progress for quality, scheduling, and cost elements.

- Monitor and process change requests.

- Assess team performance.

- Decide whether any contingency plans need to be deployed.

You will begin to execute the plan now. Your first step is to create the draft of the deliverable.

Schedule your first team meeting as a "kickoff" meeting and bring enthusiasm. Congratulate your team for the hard work. Perhaps bring in some sort of treat. You will want to motivate them toward the project with the highest possible energy.

Give your team members permission to proceed and to start interviewing each other to determine the key composites of their job duties. Summarize your deliverables for the team. Review the schedule and the activity list together. Go over the quality plan one final time and then give them verbal or written permission to begin the project. Say when you will meet again as a team, if you have a regular status meeting planned, and what will be expected to be completed by then.

As the project is underway, you might find opportunities to provide training for some of your team members. Unless a member is doing exactly the same task as he or she does in a normal workday, chances are good that someone is going to be learning something new. The person might take to it naturally or might require assistance.

For instance, suppose one of the people on the team is required to use Microsoft Excel and has never done so before. You will want to provide time for that person to go through the built-in tutorial or similar training.

As you use the Management By Walking Around style, be especially aware of areas where people are struggling and consider whether training would be a solution.

Be aware that appreciation is a huge motivator, so look for areas where people are excelling. Have a formal recognition of at least one individual in your regular status meetings. In between meetings, when you see people doing something well, tell them.

Progress Reports

You will comprise much of your progress reports from information obtained in your meetings. At each status meeting, you will want to review the scope of your project carefully. Review the action items, line by line, and evaluate the progress. Are the deliverables being created at the quality levels you decided were required? Are they being completed on time? Are the key milestones being met, or are things taking longer than you expected? Were your resources underestimated? What about your costs? How do the actuals compare to what you had estimated?

You will find variances as you proceed. Your job is to evaluate them for impact. If they are small and you can adjust things to adapt for the variance, do so. If they are large enough that they will compromise the project's scope, such as your schedule will extend past the end date or the budget will be higher than anticipated, you will need to meet with your sponsor. Explain to the sponsor the background, the problem, and your recommendations.

CASE STUDY: JOSEPH ZUBAY

Joseph Zubay is one of the founders of LinkIndigo Company, a consulting firm out of Illinois. For the past eight years, he has consulted with project managers about how to manage their projects for maximum effectiveness. He explains how important it is to go to your sponsor with this kind of information right away:

"When we do our estimates for costs, we use both bottom-up and top-down

---

CASE STUDY: JOSEPH ZUBAY

methods. We try to make a judgment in the middle. As we look back at our success, we find that our estimates come in pretty close. Over the years, you can get closer and closer. You want to take your most experienced people and put them in the cost-estimating arena. It takes a lot of judgment to put costs together.

"If variances arise and they are significant, you need to utilize your communication skills with middle and top management and see how you can negotiate the best bailout. See what they will do about changing budget or moving the goalposts. If you get yourself into a tight spot, do not stay there. As soon as you discover it, get it out in the open. Get with the people who can help. If it costs you your job, okay, but you might save some other people. Most of the time, you will be better off, as a result."

As you step through your meeting, create or update your issues list. If you have any open issues from a former meeting, get a status from your team about the progress made on them. Which ones are resolved, and what is needed to resolve the others? Cross off the ones you have completed, but leave them on the list. This visual of progress will be motivating to you and the team.

Likewise, you always want to keep people focused on the schedule. As each activity is completed, you update the schedule. If an activity needs to be extended, change the schedule with your team's buy-in, provided it does not compromise your constraints.

Each meeting should also touch on a review of your team's risk management plan. It will likely need to be modified as you progress, and you might have new risk items to add. Suppose you find out that the binder you were planning to use is back-ordered for another 60 days? What is your backup plan? Add it to your risk plan. For example, "When we are ready to begin binding the final document, if you find that the binder we selected is still out of stock, we will use the next size larger. This will cost $x more than we anticipated, which is still within the project's budget."

Let us address the situation where your individual team members cannot come to an agreement about how to proceed on a particular issue. We will not call this an argument; suppose we have strong reasons why one group of people cannot come around to what a different group recommends, and suppose this lack of resolution is preventing you from moving forward on your schedule. How can you handle that?

CASE STUDY: SARY MABJISH

Sary Mabjish has a system in his environment whereby he makes attempts to resolve within the team, but when he cannot, he will escalate. He describes it as follows:

"If there is discord, as a project manager, I try to resolve within the team and find the most efficient way. If we reach a point where meeting after meeting we are at the same standoff, then we escalate to the steering committee, a group of higher- level managers, including the sponsor, who can step in with their decision.

"We introduce it to them as, 'We are not reaching a decision on this issue, and we need to take it up with you.' Sometimes they ask for more documentation prior to their decision and, of course, we provide it. Then, when the decision comes, we take it back to the project team and stakeholders and advise the decision has been made."

At the conclusion of your meeting, be sure to have your meeting minutes published, along with your progress report that should clearly define any issues or action items. You want to make sure everyone knows who is responsible for what, by when, and that this information is published within your team by the end of the day.

Between meetings, you will continue to oversee the interviews, the typing of each position's duties, and other action items by using other means of communication, such as e-mail. It is helpful if you are able to track your progress in some sort of recordable format. Suppose you are walking around and Joe tells you that he just found a new source for the same size binder you were going to use before. This is good news, and you will want to make a record of it. Even though you and Joe just made a decision to change your risk management plan to reflect this change, the rest of the team does not yet know this. Plus, you always want to have an audit trail of your decisions.

In this case, you can go back to your office and send a quick e-mail out to the group about Joe's find and the subsequent decision to change the risk plan. In your memo, you direct the appropriate person on the team to update the risk plan by the end of the day. Then, you add this item to the project's activity list. By the time your next status meeting is held, this action item should be completed, and everyone will know why and what happened. Because you provided it in writing, the responsible party cannot say, "Well, I did not know I had to do that."

CASE STUDY: PEGGY SANCHEZ

"Project managers need to have a unique set of skills that include keeping people motivated, relating well to them, and constantly updating them via effective communication. That is hard to do.

"I have learned to put everything in writing, and in our company, we use a Web-based program called TWiki (**www.twiki.org**). It is like a bulletin board. When someone says, 'Well, I did not know about that,' I can say, 'It was on the board.' People will sometimes come to meetings with attitudes and say, 'That is not my job,' and I just laugh. They spend more time on thinking about how not to do things than to just get the task list done." The key is to record absolutely everything you expect to get done and everything that has been accomplished.

Between meetings, if your team runs into any issues, you need to facilitate their resolution or delegate this task to the team leader or your assistant. You need to run interference for your team members and allow them to breeze through the projects as easily as possible, especially if they also have other duties.

Change Requests

Prepare for change. We have already shown how scope creep can be a big risk to your project schedule. When you are managing multiple projects, it is even more important that you control the changes as much as possible. Whereas in a single project, scope creep happened because people came and cajoled their issues into your project, when managing multiple projects, it happens of its own accord. It happens because you add a little here and someone else adds a little there. Your own team might be at fault without realizing it. For instance, someone in word processing who sees all the work piling up might take it upon herself to accept more work from someone else and not tell you. It becomes a matter of, "Oh what the heck, one more thing will not matter at this point," and you realize that you have 15 percent more activities on your list than you had planned.

Stay calm. Recognize that you need to address the cause of the problem and the problem itself.

In the above example, the word processor did not follow the predetermined process about how change requests were to be processed, nor did the other people who added a bit here and there. When you discover something of this nature, it substantiates an emergency meeting with your team. You need to tell them the problem, why it happened, and how it needs to be modified, immediately. You need to exercise caution when identifying why the problem happened because you never want to give anyone negative feedback in public. You do not want to say something like, "We are in over our heads because Renee decided to be nice and take on extra work. Bless her heart, she meant well, but it has put us in a bind." Although you may be disappointed with Renee, take that on privately, if you feel it warrants it.

For the team, your approach to the problem should be stated as, "All right team, I just became aware that we are experiencing an alarming amount of scope creep in our project, and I wanted to pull you together to address it. We have to be careful to follow the scope changes that we put into place and not accept any more work from anyone on this project without going through the process, even if it is the vice president. Do you understand? I will tell him about this issue and how I have directed you to pay particular attention to this and that even he has to fill out the forms if he wants to add something to this project. What are your questions or concerns about this?"

Be sure to ask that open-ended question at the end of your directive rather than something people can just reply to with yes or no. You want to draw them in. You expect them to have questions or concerns. One of the questions might be "What happened? Who took on more work?" Your answer: "That does not matter right now. We need to address the situation we have and not get into blame mode."

Next, you will need to address the impact of the problem to your project. You will evaluate your contingency plan. Had you already planned for something similar to what you are facing? Can the solution be found by implementing the contingency plan? If so, that may be what you will want to recommend to your sponsor.

If not, you need to comprise a new recommendation and modify your existing contingency plan. It may be that the extra work is enough to drive you to ask for more time, more resources, more budget, or some sort of concession about the final deliverable. You decide what you need, exactly, with your team. Then, you will meet with your sponsor and make a case for your request. You will identify the issues that brought about the need for change. You will present its impact and identify the changes to the schedule, budget, resources, or other factors, clearly but briefly. Upon his or her acceptance of your changes, update your schedules and other project data.

Should your sponsor not approve of the changes, it may be that your project is over. Let us evaluate when it might be time to abandon your project. This decision normally comes with much emotion, and you will need to rely on your project management skills. One of the project managers we interviewed summarized a set of skills that would apply well to a situation such as this.

CASE STUDY: MIKE HEUTMAKER

"A good project manager needs to have a unique set of skills. Organization is at the top. Another key is the ability to maintain steady thinking under pressure. He or she needs clear vision of the company's expectations and the ability to consider how a decision they make will impact other objectives the company may have in place.

"One very useful asset is a thick skin. The project manager will often take the heat for something that he or she had nothing to do with but is the middleman.

"When your sponsor and the whole team are going to react strongly over abandoning a project, you need to be sure that thick skin is zipped up tight."

Abandoning a Project

One of the most difficult decisions you will make is to close down an unfinished project. It is human nature to hang on and believe something cosmic is about to happen that will fix all the problems. Your momentum is rolling, your team is committed, and your emotion is high over the idea of abandoning it.

Yet, there are conditions when it is the right thing to do for the business. Your company might have its own criteria, but a common list of these types of conditions are as follows:

- **When your sponsor withdraws.** Obviously, this one that trumps every argument. If you lose your sponsor's support, it is over. Close it up and move on.

- **When it no longer has value to your company.** Suppose you are in the middle of your project to build the boilerplate of products for the sales people when it is announced that your company is being bought out by another. By the end of the year, some of your products are going to be renamed or otherwise adapted, but no one knows which ones yet. It would not make sense for you to keep up with this project.

- **When the deliverables fail to materialize.** In the examples we have used, this particular condition may not arise. However, you might see how this situation would be common if you were writing software. Perhaps you are given a project to create a robot that can fly a plane. That deliverable might fail to materialize when you try to combine robotics with autopilot systems. It might happen eventually, but it would not be easy.

- **When the deliverables are continually over budget or behind schedule.** The project managers we spoke with were quick to cite poor planning as the number one reason projects fail. Chances are that if your project is over budget or behind schedule, consistently or significantly, your project's design is to blame. Before you abandon this project, you will want to evaluate your contingency plans, try to make modifications to the resource pool or budget, consult with subject matter experts or mentors, and talk with your immediate manager.

A good project manager is dedicated to the craft and will view project abandonment as a personal failure, even after years of doing the work.

We heard things like, "There is no failing in my business. I like to work smart, as well as hard."

This is admirable and an obvious sign of a strong work ethic. Of course, you will strive to make your project successful, but you must remember that you and your team are human and that project failure is not a failure if it is the right business decision.

When you make the decision to abandon the project, understand it is in the best interest of the business. Here are some comments from project managers who have had to kill a project, and they might put this concept into perspective for you:

CASE STUDY: BOB ECKERT

"We have had to abandon a project a few times over the years. It brings on mixed emotions. People are relived that the project is over, especially if it has been a troubled project, and some people feel disappointment because they might have spent a good deal of time on the project and they could not bring it to closure. But it is always the right decision."

CASE STUDY: PEGGY SANCHEZ

"It kills morale. Fortunately, when we abandoned our project, we had not gotten very far. We were doing three variations. The upper and lower ends fell into the margins, but the middle one did not. We needed to abandon it because the deliverable would not have fallen within specifications."

CASE STUDY: BINH VO

"When we approach a point where we need to abandon a project, it will come at the recommendation of the entire team. We communicate constantly with the sponsor as the project unfolds, so it is not usually a big surprise.

"Still, when you meet with the sponsor, you want to go in with your recommendation to abandon with all the facts. Tell him or her the situation and your recommendation that the project should end, as well as the other options.

Explain what it would take to keep the project going. Usually, it requires too much money or time, so the decision is obvious, but you never want to second-guess your sponsor. Always bring in all the options.

"Whatever your sponsor agrees to do, whether it is to abandon the project or allocate additional resources, be sure to get sign-off from him, plus all other key people, such as other customers."

If you do abandon your project, you still will want to go through the close-out phase, which is presented in Chapter 9.

For our purposes, we will assume your project is not abandoned and continue working toward your deliverable of a first draft of the employee handbook. You steadily work the activity list and keep a close watch on the quality, costs, schedule, scope creep, or other variances. You find yourself crossing the first milestone at the end of May, a couple of days ahead of schedule, when the first draft finally comes together.

You meet with the team, review the draft, then meet with your sponsor. The sponsor reviews it and makes suggestions for the changes he wants to see. In this same meeting, your sponsor signs off that this phase is closed and authorizes you to proceed to Phase IV.

Chapter 8

Communicate With The Tower

We are now ready to create the actual deliverable. You will meet with your team and review the changes that your sponsor recommended. Together, you will evaluate the effect of the changes to the project's costs, schedule, quality, and risks. You will continue to have regular status meetings to track your progress, throughout this phase. You will also remain in communication with others using the same formats you used before.

Phase IV: Create the Deliverables

Controls

In this chapter, we will focus on controlling the deliverable. We will pay particular attention to the variances and work to control them. You may also wish to take your control skills to the next level and learn how to use a control tool known as Earned Value Management (EVM). We will touch on this analysis technique in this chapter, as well.

Initiate Phase IV

As in the former phases, when we closed down the last phase, we received authorization to begin this one. You announce the new phase at your status meeting, along with the changes that your sponsor has requested.

Plan Phase IV

You and your team evaluate the changes that your sponsor requested. In our example, our sponsor has been the vice president of the region and certainly someone whom we want to keep happy. However, your responsibility as project manager is to ensure that any change that imposes itself onto a project will not disturb its constraints to a degree that the project fails, even if those changes come with a powerful reason to accept them.

Go through the same analysis that you would for any change to your project. You evaluate the impact to the costs, schedule, and resources required. Will these changes be part of what you were planning to do anyway? For instance, are they merely changes to the text, which is already typed and can be easily modified? Or are the changes more widespread, such as his desire that you include job descriptions of all employees: the sales people, the data manager, the sales managers, the quality manager, the operations manager, and even his own job? That would be enough to change your scope; it would be the equivalent of doing the same project again but with different people. You will need to calculate how many days this will require, which people will represent each job title, and who will do the interviews. You will want to consider where this information might already be started. Would the human resources manager have this data contained within the job descriptions that she uses when she advertises for open positions?

You will consider the entire impact to the project, then return to your sponsor and have a follow-up discussion. Present him with the costs and schedule, and get his decision on whether you should continue or not — along with your recommendation. In this instance, you encourage him to discard the idea of extending the handbook to include all the jobs. You point out that the purpose of this deliverable was to provide cross-training within the support group and to minimize the impact of vacant positions. You suggest that by incorporating sales positions into the book, you are running the risk of the book possibly walking out the door as people leave, since there is regular turnover in sales. This might compromise the proprietary nature of some of the content. For instance, how would the vice-present react if the book, which contained a description of his actual job duties, fell into the hands of an outside recruiter, and ultimately, the competition?

Your sponsor explains that he wants to make the handbook available to the sales people so they understand the work flow of the support staff and can better plan their time. He wants them to be aware of which supplies we use and how we go about getting them so they know it will take two weeks to get a new pager, for instance. He had recommended that you include their positions, also, because he thought it would be a means to incorporate them, too. However, after listening to your reasoning, he agrees with your points and withdraws the request to include them. He still would like them to receive a copy of the book, however.

You point out that there are sensitive items in the handbook, such as account numbers to order computers or passwords to get into reports systems. You continue to talk it out with him and decide that you will create two versions of the book. One is the original handbook you had set out to create; the second is an abridged version, with sensitive data removed. The second version will be distributed to the sales staff.

You go back to your team and evaluate the changes. You determine that the costs will increase over budget by nearly $1,000. Extra supplies plus extra personnel dedicated to the project comprise the additional costs. You also assess you will require three more business days to copy the extra books.

You meet with your sponsor again. He says he wants the project completed by June 30 because he wants to introduce it at a meeting in early July. As such, he allocates an additional resource to your team and loans you someone from another department to help you, however you need. You and he both sign off on the changes and you modify your project plan and scope.

Execute Phase IV

You continue, now with your focus on both releasing version two of the book, due in about ten days, and the changes your team will make to the handbook to make it suitable for release.

You and your team decide to treat the second deliverable as a subproject. A subproject is a group of activities that comprise a project in their own right but are a part of the main project. You create its own WBS, identifying that a precedent is the second version of the book. So, you prepare to launch the subproject on the day the second version is approved.

Donna is the data manager's assistant whom your sponsor allocated to you. Your team decides she would be best used as a word processor. With her help, you expect you can trim two days off the delivery date of the second version. You continue until the second version is ready for review, meeting with your team to control any variances and manage risk.

Effective Control Tools

We have stressed the importance of monitoring the progress of your project in terms of the schedule, budget, quality, and risk. We will now suggest how you might do so by offering tools to use.

There is no right or wrong answer regarding how you will keep your project aligned. Some people use project management software to show them variances; others use Microsoft Excel or Apple Numbers software, and still others use Web-based bulletin boards. In the end, it does not matter whether you use Post-It® notes all over your desk or write the back of an envelope, as long as it works for you.

For our purposes, we will offer tools that were created in Microsoft Excel, some that came to us from the project managers with whom we spoke. One of the advantages of using a spreadsheet program is that you can create it to your exact terms, and if you are advanced in Excel, you can create embedded worksheets, formulas, and graphs that will tell you how things are progressing.

Control Phase IV

Controlling the activities. As we evaluated the various tools available for tracking activities, we found an exceptional worksheet as provided by Michael Greer in his book, *The Manager's Pocket Guide to Project Management.* Look at the example in Figure 8-1, which is our modification to Mr. Greer's worksheet.

FIGURE 8-1

Worksheet: Variance Analyzer

Phase:V	Primary Resource:	Est. Days	Act. Days	Var. Days	Est. Hrs.	Act. Hrs	Var. Hrs.	Est. $$	Act. $$	Var. $$	Explanation
Activities:											
Controlled rollout.	All			0	4	3	1	$150	$113	-$37	
Test the document.	All	2		2	4	0	4	$784	$627	-$157	
Project team meeting.	All			0	0.5	0.5	0	$175	$175	$0	
Meet with Sponsor.	Mgr, Sponsor			0	1	1.5	-0.5	$60	$90	$30	Sponsor moved mtg
				0			0			$0	
TOTAL				2			4.5			-$164	

This worksheet provides a snapshot of all the activities, at a glance. It tells you which phase, which activity, the variances in duration, hours, and costs, as well as a brief explanation of the corresponding issues.

You can build in formulas that will automatically sum each category and then the entire total, as we have done.

Controlling the Schedule. We have heard that many project managers find the scheduling feature in Microsoft Project to be quite effective. There are numerous software applications available to you for no charge. We will go over this in detail in Chapter 11.

You will want a tool to help you see the variances between where you expect to be and where you are. Depending on how much detail you require, an effective tool to analyze your schedule might be attained by simply modifying the previous spreadsheet:

FIGURE 8-2

Worksheet: Variance Analyzer

Phase:V Activities:	Primary Resource:	Est. Days	Act. Days	Var. Days	Est. Hrs.	Act. Hrs.	Var. Hrs.	Est. $$	Act. $$	Var. $$	Est. Start Date	Act. Start Date	Var. Start Date	Est. End Date	Act. End Date	Var. End Date	Explanation
Controlled rollout.	All			0	4	3	1	$150	$113	-$37	6/11/08	6/11/08	0	6/11/08	6/11/08	0	
Test the document.	All	2		2	4	0	4	$784	$627	-$157	6/11/08	6/11/08	0	6/13/08	6/13/08	0	
Project team meeting.	All			0	0.5	0.5	0	$175	$175	$0	6/16/08	6/16/08	0	6/16/08	6/16/08	0	
Meet with Sponsor.	Mgr, Sponsor			0	1	1.5	-0.5	$60	$90	$30	6/17/08	6/18/08	-1	6/17/08	6/18/08	-1	Sponsor moved mtg
				0			0			$0			0			0	
TOTAL				2			4.5			-$164			-1			-1	

Earned Value Management

One control measure is so powerful that it bears discussing on its own: Earned Value Management, or EVM.

Wikipedia is a free Web-encyclopedia located at **http://en.wikipedia. org**. If you travel there and type in "Earned Value Management" you will find this definition:

"Earned Value Management (EVM) is a project management technique that seeks to measure forward progress in an objective manner. EVM is touted as having a unique ability to combine measurements of technical performance (i.e., accomplishment of planned work), schedule performance (i.e., behind/ahead of schedule), and cost performance (i.e., under/over budget) within a single integrated methodology. Proponents also claim that it provides an early warning of performance problems.

Additionally, EVM promises to improve the definition of project scope, prevent scope creep, communicate objective progress to stakeholders, and keep the project team focused on achieving progress."

This particular method is somewhat complex and relies on formulas. If you are a natural mathematician, you will find it simple. Otherwise, it may take a little practice to master. Again, there are software applications specific to project management that have EVM analysis tools built in. You will find much material about this on the Web. For instance, NASA offers a free tutorial about EVM at **http://evm.nasa. gov/definition1a.html**.

Using EVM will help you determine a more accurate estimate of cost and schedule variances; it will also provide you with a total estimate of what your project will cost if you continue without making changes.

EVM calculates costs by comparing the difference between your planned costs and actual costs by using a formula. The components of the formula are:

Planned Value (PV): The budgeted amount that was approved for a particular activity on the WBS, during a specified period. (Example: Our budget is $10,000 for six weeks, or $5,000 for the first three.)

Actual Cost (AC): The actual costs incurred for the work done on an activity, during a specified period. (Example: Our first three weeks incurred expenses of $6,000.)

Earned Value (EV): The budgeted amount for the amount of work performed, during a specified period. (Example: Our hours worked and resources used should have cost $6,500.)

To determine the **Cost Variance (CV)**, apply the formula:

CV = EV - AC.

To find the cost variance, deduct the actual costs from the budgeted costs. If you have a negative number, you are over budget.

In our example, we anticipated a budget of $5,000 for half of a project. We determined that we have spent $6,000. Our formula would look like this:

CV = $5,000 - $6,000.

CV = -$1,000

*** CV is negative; we are over budget. ***

To determine the **Cost Variance Percentage (CVP)**, use:

CVP = CV / EV x 100.

To determine the **Schedule Variance (SV)**, apply the formula:

SV = EV - PV.

To find the schedule variance, we take the difference between the amount we budgeted for the work we planned to do from the budgeted amount for what we completed.

In our example, we expected to spend $6,500 on the work we did in the first three weeks. However, we had budgeted $5,000 for this period. Our formula would look like this:

SV = $6,500 - $5,000

SV = $1,500

*** SV is positive; we are ahead of schedule. ***

To determine the **Schedule Variance Percentage (SVP)**, use:

SVP = SV / PV x 100

Now, it is time to apply the formulas we used to help us see how our project will end up, if there are no changes made to scheduling or budgeting. To find this, we use one final formula to derive the **Estimate at Completion (EAC)**.

To determine Estimate at Completion (EAC), use:

EAC = AC / EV x Total Budget

In our example, this formula would reveal the following:

EAC = $6,000 / $6,500 x $10,000

EAC = $9,230

This indicates that if all things trend as they are today, we will finish our project on time, spending less than the entire budgeted amount.

Earned Value Management is designed to help the project manager identify trends, early on, in complex projects. As your project management skills grow, make it a point to use this powerful tool.

Close Phase IV

Gather all your documentation that you are tracking, such as your WBS, change requests, variance reports, and invoices that need to be paid (relative to the project). You review the status of your project as you seek to close this phase.

You and your team will record any lessons learned where you had particular difficulties or successes. Make notes of the items you learned and will want to implement in other projects. Make payments to outside vendors, review the change order requests, and update the schedules and action items as you work to close down any issues you can.

Update your progress report to list the state of the deliverables and any accomplishments you have achieved since the last report, and mention the activities upcoming in the next phase, emphasizing the ones that will bring challenges or special requirements. Itemize any unresolved issues or attach your issues list along with your recommendations for each item.

Chapter 9

Happy Landings

This chapter will take you through the actual execution of the final deliverable and closing of the project. You will test-market your deliverable, modify it as necessary, then deploy it. You will ask your sponsor to confirm that the contract terms were met and formally accept the results of your project. You will write recommendations to your company and conduct team evaluations, then officially terminate your project, update the records, and prepare them for archiving.

Phase V: Test-Market & Release the Deliverables to Market

Initiate Phase V

When we closed down the last phase, we received authorization to begin this one. You announce the new phase at your status meeting, along with what you intend to accomplish in this final phase.

Plan Phase V

By now, there will be little planning necessary. The final two phases are spent primarily in execute and control. For planning, you simply want to review your objectives and review your documents to plan how to resolve any open items. Your objectives in this phase are to test-market, make final modifications, release the deliverable, and close the project.

Test-market the Deliverable

In most instances, before a product is released to the public, it is test-marketed.

Consider that Hollywood producers, as they manage the multimillion dollar movie business, will regularly release a motion picture in three stages. First, they will look at it in-house. Not only will they evaluate the "dailies" (the production of the movie that was filmed or edited that day), they will review the entire film before they release it to the second stage. The next group that will review the motion picture is the test audience. Audiences are selected to view the motion picture in a theater and offer their comments about it. These comments are carefully considered by the producers as they decide whether they will rewrite, refilm, or re-produce a part of the film. Either they take it back into production or release it, as is. Only after this testing is completed will the product be marketed to the public.

Project deliverables are no different. You want to first offer your deliverable to a limited group before release, and you want to be certain to build in enough time so you can react if the test market produces a need for multiple changes.

CASE STUDY: BINH VO

Binh Vo cautions new project managers to build in adequate time for testing:

"Many project managers overlook adding the time needed for testing. There are three levels of testing — four if you are working on an upgrade.

"In the example of deploying new software, the first level is done by the developers. They write a piece of functionality for the program itself and make sure it works properly. Second, a third-party, non-biased group called Software Quality Assurance (SQA) runs test cases against the software. These tests are done against the functional requirements. Third is user-acceptance testing (UAT).

CASE STUDY: BINH VO

"This kind of testing assures your product is tested at the highest level of quality. The first two groups might believe it is quality because it passed our internal tests, but when it gets to the real world, the end users are the ones who are going to use it. And they might use it in ways we never would as programmers and developers. A programmer's perception is completely different from an end-user's. And although the quality assurance people made sure all the components are there, they have no idea how it is going to be used. Internal testing does not link to external uses. You have to let the testing get out to the end-users.

"Then, I am certain that I will deliver a quality product, and at the end of the day, the person who has to love it is my customer (sponsor). He will judge the team as successful. "

In our example, we planned to test-market the deliverable by using it within the support organization. We are still following the plan we created in Phase I, and we budgeted time and resources for this activity.

We allowed for half a day for the handbook to be deployed to and reviewed by the support staff in a meeting. You may have noticed from the control tool charts that this task was completed in three hours. Your team would have simply stepped through the activity list that they had created. If you were to describe the test, your notes might read something like this:

"People received the handbooks, read it as an entire team, and asked each other questions about how each person's job was performed. Examples of potential problems or pitfalls were discussed.

"For the next two and a half days, everyone rotated into every other job other than his or her own. We had prepared a simulated set of tasks for each job, expressly for this purpose. For instance, for the word processors, the simulator demonstrated how to type a letter, a spreadsheet, a presentation document, and sales documents, such as a Request for Proposal. It showed the user how to add paper to and change toner in the printer. For the IT support person, the simulator walked the user through the ways to handle new equipment requests for laptops, printers, cell phones, and other hardware the sales people use. It showed how to distribute those same items when they arrive. It included how to handle requests for repairs and other support issues.

"By the time everyone was done, we had each had a chance to sit in each other's chair for part of a day, including mine. It was especially interesting to observe how each person reacted to wearing the manager's skill set for a while. It was insightful to see who might be a good candidate for a protégé.

"The entire simulator took only two days instead of two and a half, as we had planned. We discovered this was a flaw in the schedule. Some of the positions took less than we had anticipated and rather than just have someone idly sit there, waiting for the next tour, we bumped it up. There were other positions where we did not leave enough time, however. The word processors produce so many varied types of documents that it was nearly impossible for the visitor to test out all aspects of their work. If another region does this project, they should balance the time better during the testing."

In our project example, the next steps we would take would be to test-market the second deliverable, the salesperson's version, with a sales employee. Then, when all the feedback is gathered and the test marketing is complete, you create the final deliverable.

In this example, two key items were among the recommendations. One came from your team — that the exercise of swapping jobs needs to be done regularly. They recommend this as a monthly exercise, combined with some sort of fun activity, like a potluck lunch. Since this decision is entirely within your realm, you agree to it, and you will write it into the plan.

The other suggestion that arose was that the vice president share the deliverables with the three other regions in the company. You and your team believe that this product is so beneficial that it should be shared so that others might benefit from it. You also believe this will reflect well on your own organization. You agree to take the action item to include that in your final recommendations.

Execute and Control Phase V

You will execute the deployment of the deliverables and the closure process of the phase.

Prepare for Final Deliverables

As before, you will meet with your sponsor before releasing the final deliverable. You give him the opportunity to review the products and offer any additional changes he may want. In this case, he is satisfied with the product and signs off for you to release the final deliverables to the appropriate personnel.

Your team copies and distributes the employee handbook for the support staff to its members and the salesperson's versions to the sales teams. As both project manager and support manager, you have written an introductory letter to each person, on behalf of your team, describing the purpose of the document and welcoming them to contact you with questions.

Prepare for Closure

You have now introduced your final deliverable to the market. It is time to close down the remainder of your project, most of which is administrative in nature. In some organizations, there is a separate team, referred to as the termination team. This group is responsible for closing down the administrative details of a project, sometimes referred to as a punch list.

For our purposes, we will assume there is no termination team in place and closing out the entire project is your responsibility. Once again, you gather all your documents together and meet with your team. Now, all your task items and change requests should be shown as complete, and the schedule is at its end. You compute the final hours worked and associated costs. You either pay the outside bills, or prepare the bills to be processed appropriately. You report these and other like costs into your project. If there are any outstanding requests associated with the outside vendors, such as a need to sign off on a contract, you will attend to those matters now, too.

Close Phase V

The actual closure of Phase V should happen quickly. By now, you have completed all the tasks associated with the activities list. All that is remaining is to:

- Complete all your open documents and prepare them for archiving.

- Write evaluations of the team members.

- Write your summary and recommendations to the sponsor and other key stakeholders.

- Obtain written acceptance from your sponsor that the project is closed.

Terminating Your Project

Close your documents. Go through all your documents and wrap them up. It is likely that the ones that will require the most lead time involve paying other vendors. You want to be able to say in your final report that everything is paid. Delegate as much as possible for two reasons. First, you want to help your team members expand their skills. Second, having at least one other set of eyes on the documents will lend assuredness that things are closed. Of course, in your final team meeting, the entire group will concur that everything is wrapped up.

Write evaluations of the team members. This activity is a matter of personal preference. Some project managers will perform this function, and others will not. Of the ones who do not, they cite that the team members are not their direct reports and they do not have the authority to write formal evaluations.

In this instance, a formal evaluation is not a multiple-page document that will take you two days to write. The document is normally a page long, and you need spend only five to ten minutes completing it. We believe that this task is important and you should do it, even if your team members are not your direct reports. The reasons that you would do this include:

- It is beneficial for the team members to receive the feedback.

- Your assessment of an individual's work on the project will allow his or her manager to use your comments in the individual's annual performance appraisal.

- If you work with the team member again, he or she will be more likely to realize that you are paying attention to how things are accomplished.

Karen Thomas has been using a one-page team evaluation form for years. She was kind enough to share it with us, provided as Figure 9-1.

FIGURE 9-1

TEAM MEMBER EVALUATION FORM

Team member: _____ Project Manager: _____

Project: _____ Date: _____

Item	Poor	Fair	Good	Very Good	Excel-lent	n/a	Comments: Strengths, Weaknesses
Quality of work performed on project							
Timeliness of project task completion							
Contribution to meeting product cost and project budget targets							
Contribution to team meetings							
Cooperation with other team members							
Communication of progress, status, issues							
Communication on technical matters							
Overall performance on project							
Commendable contributions/strengths							
Major areas for improvement							
Other comments:							

If you elect not to complete an individual team evaluation form, you will at least want to write a personalized letter of thanks to each team member. Do not create a form letter for this activity. You want to make a comment specific to each person's behavior. You will copy each functional manager.

You should also consider asking your team members to evaluate you. You want to make certain you are being as effective as possible. In Sary Madjish's environment, the company instills this standard. He explains:

CASE STUDY: SARY MADJISH

"In addition to the survey that I use to evaluate the team members, we also have a survey for the team members to evaluate the project manager. The questions ask things such as 'Were they satisfied? Did they think the project manager was involved to the extent he should have been?

CASE STUDY: SARY MADJISH

"Did they think the project manager was helpful? Knowledgeable? Did the job he was supposed to do?' This document does not come to us — it comes to our boss. If there are issues, the boss talks to us. Management wants to know you are involved."

Summary and recommendations. You will update your status report one final time to address the following items:

- Say the accomplishments you attained in the final phase.

- Confirm that the deliverables you described in the project charter have been attained or, if the sponsor approved changes to it along the way, that the desired outcome was produced.

- Say that all issues are resolved and all activities are closed.

- Say that all bills are paid, contracts closed, and expenses and work hours loaded.

   ° Provide a total cost of the project. Compare the number to the original budget and explain any minor variance. (Any major variance would have been addressed before now.)

   ° Do the same exercise with the scheduling by comparing the actual days/hours worked against the projected ones.

- Comment on whether any of your anticipated risks arose or if you had to use any contingency plans.

- Make final recommendations to the sponsor.

   ° Release the deliverable to the other regions

- Recognize your team members and comment about any particularly effective person or people, along with a brief description of their contribution.

- Request final sign-off from the sponsor on a separately attached document.

By listing the information above, you have effectively created your completion report. The document will be used to report the completion of the project, and you will use it to request the project be closed. Simply remove the first bullet item (say the final phase's accomplishments), change the title to the project name and dates worked, and you have a good completion report.

You will meet with your team one final time to review your status report and recommendations. If the team has no additional input, you will meet with your sponsor to request that the project be closed.

Accept the Results of the Project

When you meet with your sponsor, you will want to provide him with three documents. The first is your final status report that you will review with him. This document should be attached to the second document — the project charter.

By bringing the charter into the closure meeting, you can ensure that everything you agreed to do initially has been done or can be accounted for. Sary Mabjish emphasizes how this works quite well:

CASE STUDY: SARY MABJISH

"The charter goes side by side with the completion report. The completion report will address the charter — did we meet our deadline? Did we go over budget? We also include recommendations about what happened and how it can be improved."

The final document you will bring with you is the project sign-off form. This is a document that your sponsor will sign stating the he has reviewed the stated deliverables. He indicates whether he gives complete approval or whether there are any exceptions to his approval. If there are exceptions, he will list what they are. He gives approval for the next step of the product that you produced. In our example, he would hand it over to you, as support manager, to proceed with updating it as you decided. In many instances, the sponsor will give approval for the product to be delivered to another department for further development. You want your sign-off document to contain a clause indemnifying your sponsor from future changes to the product, after it leaves his scope of influence. He will sign it and date it, and you are officially done with your project.

Part 3

Rocket Tools: Propel Your Project Management Skills to the Stratosphere

In Part 2, we stepped through the process of managing a project, using our simulated example of creating an employee handbook. Throughout the process, our schedule and resources were virtually flawless. No one quit during the middle of it, nothing malfunctioned, and our sponsor and manager was always available for us, if needed.

That scenario is rare. More common is the likelihood that you, as project manager, will be engaged in multiple projects at once. Think back to our example of the Hollywood producer who is juggling several films at once. This is typical. Home builders do not build one house at a time, clothing designers do not create just one dress, and airlines do not fly just one plane.

In this section, we will define and explore the environment of managing multiple — or complex — projects. We will identify the unique risk factors that you need to understand and offer tips from actual project managers on how to be most successful as a "juggler."

Finally, we will take a high-level look at some of the software and technology that is available to assist in managing projects or pieces of projects. In addition to describing their application, we will provide you with the Web sites for all our examples to allow you to review these products more fully.

Chapter 10

Multiple Projects = Air Traffic Control

Managing complex, multiple projects is far more common in the real world than managing a single one. Until now, we have focused on a single project so we could explain each component. It is time to apply the basics to the environment you may encounter as a project manager.

Multiple projects, by definition, imply that you will manage more than one project at the same time. It could also mean that the people on your team will be part of other teams, concurrently, or that other resources might be required for more than one project. For instance, suppose your project involves real estate and you need to hire a pressure-washing machine to clean three different houses. You will need to put together a schedule to account for each house. Can you get all three done in one or two days? Are the houses too far from each other to use the resource multiple times on the same day? Or, is the general contractor who will perform the task going to bring his own equipment, and if so, can you schedule him on the same day? These kinds of questions will be common as you manage multiple projects.

A multiple or complex project might also involve having the same client or sponsor, activities, or audiences. For instance, if your audience contains the data systems manager in two separate projects, you will want to consider how to best work with her so you are not duplicating efforts. In this example, you might want to consider meeting with her to address issues from each project, simultaneously.

You do not need to change what you already have learned about project management. You will still deploy the same skills, except you will add new skills that will assist you in managing multiple or complex projects effectively.

The most critical components of your new skill set center on organization and communication. As the project manager, you will need to know the status of each activity in each project, where you are on schedule and budget, where resources are available or overburdened, and every other detail about each project. Even the more mature project management organization sometimes cannot tell how many projects it has going at one time. This is due to the multiple changes that take place during a project. For instance, if a project grows too large, it might be divided into subprojects. What was once one project is now two or even three. Furthermore, when the same resources are used concurrently in more than one project, the actual time spent on each project might not be known. If you lose track of how much time people are being used or how many projects you have, your schedules are in danger of not being met.

Project Portfolio Management (PPM): PPM is the process of managing the continuous flow of projects from concept to completion. Think of it as a group of projects that are managed by one person. This is a way to coordinate your processes to ensure your resources and priorities are most effective.

Multi-Project Analysis is a method used to analyze the impact to activities when more than one project is underway and the progress of one group affects the other, especially as it relates to groups sharing people and equipment. There are many different mechanisms to evaluate this situation, to ensure you are as effective as possible in these areas. One of the most popular is to use project management software. As we will see in the next chapter, there are more software choices available today than ever before. However, it is beneficial to first step through the elements of managing a multiple or complex project "manually" so you can best choose and use whatever software you decide to employ.

Assess the Scope of Deliverables

Whether you are working a single, simple project or complex, multiple ones, the first step is to understand your deliverable and why you are creating it. Talk with your sponsor thoroughly to ensure this deliverable or set of deliverables is the solution to the underlying problem. Ask him or her what he expects it to look like when it is completed. Of course, you do not want to do this in a challenging manner, as if your sponsor should need to substantiate the need to you. You also do not want to appear defensive or agitated — which is admittedly difficult at times. If you are already stressed from too much work, plus learning a new job, it might be easy to slip into an emotional state.

Relax. Take a deep breath. Try to remember that your sponsor may be under pressure, too, maybe even more than you are. Come about this situation a different way. Offer something like, "I understand the business need to create this product, however, I fear that we might not have adequate resources or budget to provide the deliverable you seek within the schedule you seek. Can we talk this through so I can better understand what you hope this project will provide? Then, let me do some thinking and I will come back to you with a recommendation about how we might meet all the needs of the business."

Your sponsor should be all right with such a reply, because you are not telling him or her "no," but at the same time, you are explaining you have a need to manage your business, too. This kind of due diligence might be appreciated because your sponsor will gain confidence that you not only understand the project need, but also have additional insights into the level of challenge that he or she is facing. Think about your own group that you manage. When you ask someone on your team to perform a task and that person reacts in a panic and pushes back at you that it is not possible, how does that make you feel? What kind of opinion do you have of your team member after such a demonstration? Consider instead if your team member gave you a similar answer to what we recommend, above. That might make you want to open up a little to him or her and tell more about why you need this and what is at stake. You might even gain a sense of camaraderie with your team member, because he or she took the time to understand your perspective.

Do yourself a favor. Understand what you are creating, why it is necessary, exactly what it will look like when it is done (how big, what color, what size, all the facts) and how it will fit the problem and be the ultimate and only solution before you start the planning.

Not only do you want to take time to do this for your own organizational needs, but it could happen that the product you are being asked to create is not the answer to the problem.

When we spoke with successful project managers across the country, this piece of advice came up almost universally. There were two insights that we found most memorable that we will share, below.

First, Binh Vo explained it using a metaphor that was particularly effective:

CASE STUDY: BINH VO

"Say your sponsor tells you to acquire a 2007 BMW in a week's time with a budget of $20,000. There is no reality there. You need to measure the reality. This is one pitfall that many new project managers fall into. They do not see the big picture or measure the

CASE STUDY: BINH VO

reality, because they do not know their boundaries yet. Always ask. At the end of the project, if it fails, it will reflect on you, not your sponsor.

"So, in this example, suppose the new project manager runs out and finds a 2007 BMW in a junkyard, with no tires. You go back to your sponsor and tell her you have this car without tires, kind of broken, in a junk yard. Well, you found the car, so is your project successful? Did you fix her problem? Probably not, because you never asked what it was. If she wanted to drive it to work because her car was broken, you should tell her that this requirement will not be met, unless she wants to increase the budget or give you many months to search for this deliverable. Bring her all the prices for 2007 BMWs — with tires. Ask her if she wants to meet the budget or meet the requirement. Anticipate her questions. Come in with a plan B, such as, 'Here is the price for used tires and the prices at a good body shop.'"

CASE STUDY: PAUL SCHOEN

This example came from Paul Schoen, who offered us insights about how far reaching this step can be:

"In our environment, we follow a gated approach — similar to software development. The first two gates are the business case to garner approval. Before we will even begin a project, we have a governance that has us analyze and determine the deliverable's alignment to business.

"For example, if legislature says they want everyone to be fingerprinted when they are arrested, no matter what they get arrested for, we would first look to see how that aligns to our business to determine what we would need to get through it and justify it. The second piece is to determine the necessary resources, outside entities, and staff. Only then would we start, plan, gather requirements, build, and implement it.

"If we did not take those steps, we might have immediately launched into purchasing and deploying 25 new fingerprint machines. Everyone is so quick to use technology just because it is available. Many project managers do not take the time to assess the problem, not only to make sure that the deliverable is going to fix it, but to evaluate what else you are creating with it. In this example,

CASE STUDY: PAUL SCHOEN

perhaps the problem was not that people needed to be fingerprinted; perhaps there is a flaw in the arresting process or the criminal databases. Plus, by fingerprinting everyone who is arrested, we are gathering information that judges, social workers, lawyers, and human services personnel will also acquire. We may have fixed our problem, but can we integrate our proprietary information with somebody down the line? What is the impact of that?"

After you and your sponsor agree with the exact deliverable that you will create and that this deliverable is the solution to the problem, you will consider how this new project will fit in with other projects you are managing.

If your sponsor or sponsors ask you to manage so many projects that your resources become insufficient, you will need to evaluate each project's requirements carefully. As a manager, you will be expected to make sound recommendations to your superiors, including if it is not possible to successfully overlap too many projects. Of course, you will rely on the nature of the business issue to help drive your recommendation. If your sponsor needs you to manage a project where a new child's toy is to be introduced to the market at the onset of the Christmas season, you certainly would not recommend postponing that project's start date until September. However, you might look at the projects you are currently managing and see if any of those can be interrupted and resumed later in the year.

If you are asked to take on too many projects at one time, you will want to consider your recommendation to your sponsor by using the following checklist:

- Understand each project's desired deliverable and which problem or market it intends to address.

- Evaluate each project for its own benefit and what benefits it offers others.

- Document the commitments for people and other resources on each project.

- Map each project's schedule and its associated performance, to date.

When you have considered these factors, your recommendation may pop out at you. The second bullet point is particularly important. You need to take a step back, sometimes, and see where the most people are benefited by a project. In the example we used of the toy coming out at Christmas, you may not have the option of recommending this project be postponed, but even if you did, would this project benefit the most people? A successfully selling product on the market would be more effective to the company than an employee handbook, but what if you were trying to decide between all toys? Say you worked for a toy industry and your projects were always toys, and the holiday gift-giving season is critical, every year. Which toy would you decide could be postponed, if any?

Sometimes the solution is not to postpone but to increase budget. Add more personnel so you can get all your toys to market in time for the biggest retail impact of the year.

When the day gets busy and the stress levels rise, it is all about organization and prioritization. Your sponsor might be your boss, but you work for the company, too. You need to give him or her your input about what might or might not be feasible and talk it through.

But what about those sponsors who bark a command at you, then do not want to be bothered?

We asked actual project managers whether they had experienced situations (either current or in the past) when they have had difficulty capturing their sponsor's ear about problems in providing the deliverables requested. Of the people we spoke with, only about 25 percent reported experiencing this sort of issue in their entire project management history, yet this question arises constantly from new project managers.

A handful shared their experiences about this issue, but we found that the most insightful advice came from Bob Eckert, who described dealing with this situation in a past work environment. He emphasizes that project managers need to highlight the benefits of talking through issues to their sponsors. Stress to your sponsor that these questions are not to threaten them — or waste their time — but to produce success. So how does he recommend dealing with a sponsor who is too busy to talk with you about your concerns?

CASE STUDY: BOB ECKERT

"It is not a comfortable position to be in. You know that you need their help, and they do not have time. This could impact your ability to hold the team together, especially if the decision you need the sponsor to make ties to a major deliverable that your team is working on. You have to be persistent and continue to work through them or their administrative assistant to get on their schedule. Sometimes, I found stopping by their office 'impromptu' to catch them at a good time was very effective."

CASE STUDY: DAN MASON

Dan Mason told a story about how he had trouble securing his sponsor's support on something he needed, as follows:

"When I first started, I had a manager who was sponsoring a spring sale on a bunch of condos in a new development, and it was like he could not take any time for details.

He said, 'Here, sell these over a period of days by doing this and that to launch

CASE STUDY: DAN MASON

the marketing plan.' Then he wanted to walk away. I tried to give him feedback about advertising and pricing issues, and he just said, 'Dan, just sell it.' It was very frustrating. I finally had to make my point to him by talking with a peer of his (at his same level) who made the point to him. To this day, I wonder how I could have done that better. The good news is that we got the development sold, finally. But I had to make a lot of assumptions, without his input. He wanted the result and did not care about the steps. He did not even care about the money he needed to spend. I started to wonder why I cared about his bucks when he did not.

"Then, a few months later, I got the exact opposite in managers. He is totally into support and helping. He has never let me down, except for the time he stole my favorite contractor to build a pool. I had a house that I was all set to rehab. I had all the costs done, and I asked the sponsor to let me use the best rehabber on the team. This thing could have been repaired in less than two weeks. It was mostly just paint, carpet, refinishing the floors. He said no, because he wanted (the rehabber in question) to go work on a pool project at a different site. But this rehabber was not our pool expert, and I really needed him. In the end, I had to reschedule my project to get the rehabber expert, but it ended all right. Now I tell my sponsor that he owes me for that, whenever I really need something. He is a good guy, mostly."

Before we conclude the topic about sponsors who have not been entirely perfect all the time, there is one more aspect to consider. Sometimes, people simply expect too much from their sponsor.

Some managers, especially if they are inexperienced, seek what is commonly referred to as "stroking." It may be difficult for you to self-analyze, but do evaluate whether you are asking your sponsor for a discussion over a legitimate concern or if you want something else. New managers need to accept that this kind of desire is normal, not something to be ashamed of. You are in unknown waters, and you want to do well. What better way to ask if you are doing well than to have lengthy discussions with the "big boss" to ensure there is comfort and understanding all over the place?

Keep yourself on topic by referring to the checklist, above. Keep the conversation on the business issues. While you may be the most charming person on earth, resist the instinct to compliment the sponsor about her children, his golf game, or whatever. Keep the discussion on the project, keep your questions limited to 15 seconds in length, try to keep the answers limited to two minutes, and contain the whole discussion in 15 minutes. This will help ensure you are focused on the most important matters.

Once you are comfortable in your assessment of the scope of the deliverable, prepare to evaluate the risks.

Assess Risks

Recall that a risk factor is a condition that will either produce or facilitate a risk. Can you imagine how multiple projects may complicate your risk factors? If your simple, single project is scheduled to conclude in three tight weeks, how will that change if you have six or ten more projects handed to you to complete in the same time?

- Know the basic rules about managing risk. Come to terms with what you are facing. Quantify it in terms of the actual costs to your project by estimating the extent of the consequences.

- Evaluate the number of your team's members against the number of projects they are working on and over what dates.

- Assess your dependencies in each project for cause and effect: what will happen if you pull a resource form project one to put into project two? Pay particular attention to the dependencies.

- Evaluate the human component from too many deadlines and other pressures. Be careful not to impose your own feelings here.

  ° If one of your team members intends to quit if things get any worse, will adding another project make that happen? If so, is this a person who is critical to the success of any project? Have you had this discussion with this person, or is this simply your own fear?

Use your risk-management plan when necessary after garnering the approval of key personnel, such as your sponsors and primary stakeholders.

Launch One Project Among Many

As with a single project, you went to your sponsor and other stakeholders to obtain permission to evaluate and plan. You will do so again when you launch another project while others are ensuing. If your sponsor has directed you to do it, you will not require a feasibility study, but you will still talk with him or her to define the deliverable.

Your sponsor told you to create a customer boilerplate of each of your products so that any sales person could send personalized detail as part of a sales effort. You need to ask the same questions: "How big is each boilerplate? How big is too big? Do you want it written in conversational style or more formal? Should we expect to print it in color or black and white? Do you want glossy pages? What size paper and how should it be folded? Do you want graphics included? Do you want us to fold it and use business envelopes, or should we keep it straight and mail it out in flat envelopes? Or should we use some sort of express mail, maybe even the "fake" ones that say express on the outside but are third class? Is there a cost limit to the postage? The graphics? The paper? When do you want this completed?"

Did you notice what question is missing from the above? You should have been looking for it and wondering why it was not the first one there. The question you always want to ask your sponsor is, "What is the problem, and what are we trying to resolve?"

If you speak with your sponsor about the underlying problem, you may uncover that the sales people are complaining that they do not have the time to wait for individual client letters to go out. They want something more automated. Upon further probing, you may uncover that the problem is tied to the turnaround time of your word processors. Maybe four or five key sales people complained that their sales pitches were a week late in going out. Did you just discover a different problem to this situation? Do we need to spend hundreds, perhaps thousands of dollars creating a boilerplate of potential sales documents — some of which may never be used — or is the problem that you need another word processor? Or a better one? Always ask plenty of questions before you begin. Your sponsor is your client, and you want your end product to not only fix the problem, but make him or her delighted with your team's work, too.

Assuming you discover the boilerplate is the actual solution and you are ready to proceed with the project, you will still seek to obtain the charter and introduce the project to the team. You will introduce each project separately, in its own meeting.

Manage People's Activities to Avoid Conflicts

We comprised a responsibility allocation matrix in Chapter 5. It is especially important to evaluate people's roles when they are engaged in simultaneous projects. You want to ensure there are no conflicts or that people do not become overcommitted. Although you, as manager, need to encourage your team members to work consistently and maintain their focus, you do not want to give them so much work that they can no longer prioritize.

This type of situation is what makes software ideal for project management. If your company does not use any, you may want to research the options. Some of them are free, Web-based programs. Others require that your company expend some dollars, but if you can prove that the purchase will provide savings in the long run, do it.

At the least, you should be putting your projects into some sort of a spreadsheet. The two most common are Microsoft's Excel and Apple's Numbers. With either of these applications, you can create any spreadsheet that works for you. Additionally, you can import spreadsheets that others have already created from various online options (see next chapter).

We put together Figure 10-1 below as an example of how you might build an Excel spreadsheet that will allow you to visualize who is working on which activity and step and whether that person has primary responsibility or is otherwise involved (see legend). This is a simple spreadsheet; you can create a similar one to show multiple projects.

FIGURE 10-1

Project: Employee Handbook

Activity / Step	Project Mgr	Barbara	Marcus	Laura	Arturo	Joe	Elena	Renee	Henri	Kris	Daniel	Carla	Sponsor	Manager	Vice Pres
		Project Team Members											Other Stakeholders		
A1:S1															
A1:S2															
A1:S3															
A1:S4															
A1:S5															
A2:S1															
A2:S2															
A2:S3															

PR = Primary Responsibility   SR = Supporting Responsibility   NR = Notification Required   AR = Approval Required   CR = Consultation Required   NR = Notification Required

Prepare the Statement of Work

When you prepared the Statement of Work for a single project, you looked carefully at precedents and decedents. You made sure you did not create a task such as copy the book before the task type the book. When you manage multiple projects, you will apply the same principle, except you will look between projects.

Say you have been given a project to create a boilerplate of customer proposals for the sales people. This project is similar to the employee handbook in that the final deliverable is a document. You will require some of the same resources, such as word processors, paper, toner, and finishing products. You will need some additional resources, such as product brochures, that you will insert into the document.

You will need to evaluate whether your word processors are going to be able to work on both projects simultaneously. Evaluate the hours required and evaluate the approximate start and end date. Include a description of who will be required to participate and in what capacity — how it will differ from each project. All these items need to be considered, as before, but by looking at both projects instead of one.

The same concept applies if you are working three, four, five, or more projects at once. You might see how organization is critical. What kind of skills will you require from your team members? What are the goals of each project, and are any of them related to each other? How will you be sure to capture the correct amount of time worked on each project so that you can estimate the cost of each project, especially if you run them concurrently? Are the communication tools that you currently use sufficient for managing a portfolio?

As you organize your projects, you will want to keep prioritization in mind. For instance, suppose your sponsor told you that the customer boilerplate took priority over the employee handbook. You would need to adjust your project schedule accordingly.

Prepare Work Breakdown Structure

Again, just as in a single project, you will comprise a WBS that itemizes each activity that will need to be done from start to finish, by project. Next, you will allocate and assign resources to each activity. You will level or stack them, as required. You will ensure the people or other resources that you require will be available on the days you anticipate needing them. You will calculate the initial budget and step through the project.

Interact with Other Project Members

In our example, you are the only project manager, but consider that you might be in an environment where there are several project managers within the company. If you do not interact with the other project managers, you run the risk of not heading off a potential resource crunch or other delay. Suppose another project manager is going to need a large shipment packaged and sent out around the same time you will. There is nothing more disappointing that to sweat through an entire project, get to the final step and find out there is some other person in line ahead of you and now you have to wait. If only you had known about that other person, you might have avoided the delay. That is why it is important to interact with other project managers or other managers who are using the same resources you are.

CASE STUDY: MIKE TULIPON

Mike Tulipon has managed projects in the retail industry for six years. He goes as far as to have each resource and his or her manager sign a contract with him for each project.

CASE STUDY: MIKE TULIPON

"Whenever I need to employ the same people for more than one project, I have them sign an actual contract with me, then I have their boss sign it, too. It says the project name, the task that each one will do in detail and what dates I am going to need them. If it is only for part of the day, I will put down how many hours on each day. I also have a comment on there that the person signs that states they agree to commit their time to this project, that they recognize they are working on more than one project and each one is important, and they will bring me any issues as soon as they find them, including if they are too stretched for time. I do not pull any punches with these people. I learned early on that people will whine at me about how overworked they are if I let them. I put the terms right out front. Then I get their boss to sign it, and I sign it, too.

"This may sound like I am a tough guy and do not care, but the reality is they all know I am a big softie. I just want a demonstrative thing that shows their commitment and that they know what they are getting into. I also want them to come tell me when it is too much, but only after they really think so. I do not like to change resources in the middle of a project.

"When the project is over I usually take those contracts that they signed and attach them to the attaboy letters I write at the end of the project. I usually write a great big "Thank You" diagonally across the contract when it is done. People have come to see the contracts as a good thing."

Report Progress

As project manager, it is up to you to keep people focused on their priorities. It is easy for them to get lost in the parts and lose sight of the big picture. Use your communication tools and status meetings as means to keep people focused on their goals. Show them how much progress they are making and give them warm, sincere feedback. Much of being a project manager is being a "cheerleader," as Peggy Sanchez says, in this anecdote:

CASE STUDY: PEGGY SANCHEZ

"We had a project that came up at the end of the quarter and we had only two weeks to get it done, and it was formidable. The business decision came, and we had to respond.

"We decided to switch gears on projects and get this one done, against all odds. I got a hold of people I needed and really scrambled. I used empathy and made sure everyone knew I was on the same team with them. The end of this story is that we actually got it done. It was amazing. But using motivation and showing that I believed in them was key.

"I see some people in my day-to-day world that I wish I could influence to be more positive. They have so much to offer — they have ten or even 20 more years of experience than I. I could learn so much from them, but they are typically jaded. I want to say, 'If you just changed your attitude, you would not stay in this position. You would be promoted or something. People with a negative attitude usually hold themselves back.

"I am total cheerleader. It is my nature. I think that is part of project management. You have to be sure of what you are making and that you are asking for fair things."

Change, Inevitable Change

As the project manager, you need to remember that your team members are not computers. This may sound ridiculous, but think about it. You can program a computer and then reprogram it, all day long if necessary, and it will just adapt. But try telling your team members to launch step one, activity one on project one at 9 a.m., then change it in 15-minute increments, and see how long it takes someone to blow. This is an exaggeration, but that is how it feels, sometimes, to the team members. They are working away at their task, and you come and change it a few too many times. It is difficult not to take it personally, as if they did not finish things fast enough. Worse, they will begin to lose faith in the organization, if you change things that fast — as well they should.

When managing multiple projects, change will happen exponentially, and it will take its toll on your team. Expect it. Part of your job is to evaluate any place in the project where change may arise and try to avoid it in the first place. Pay particular attention to the risk factors against the project schedule. Many project managers will add more buffer time than normal, or increase the budget, if possible. This practice is commonly referred to as padding.

We have not addressed motivation as its own art, yet, but it bears mentioning. You may not be a team member's direct manager, but you are responsible for the performance of each person. You want them to be as happy as possible. Surveys have been taken, for decades, asking people what motivates them. Even more than salary, one factor has risen to the top of the list repeatedly — appreciation.

It is so easy to show appreciation for people, and it is free. It buys you so much. You can do this in little ways, such as buying lunch for the team or giving people recognition in front of the group. If you elect to use recognition, be sure to find a way to recognize every person on your team, even if you have to search hard to find a reason for someone. Consider this example, from Binh Vo:

CASE STUDY: BINH VO

"My resources are crucial to me. I will do just about anything to show them how much I appreciate their dedication. For instance, I will bring in the cake on someone's birthday. It says you remembered, and it is a way that the whole team can come together. You also have to be willing to defend your resources. For example, suppose you are at lunch in the cafeteria, and someone is going off about how horrible Bob is and you overhear it. Bob is one of your team members, and you speak up and say, 'If you cannot say anything nice, do not say anything at all.'

"First of all, you defended a team member, which is the most important thing. Second, it might get back to Bob that you stood up for him, and others on the team might hear about it. Suddenly, you have proven yourself to be someone who will defend the team. It is amazing how much loyalty will bring you. Be loyal to your resources, always."

When your team is embroiled in multiple projects and feeling stressed, bring in ice cream for everyone and just say thank you. Tell them how much you appreciate their help. They might not show it, but it will make a difference.

Managing multiple projects means breaking more things down, paying attention to the schedule and your resources. Now that we have stepped through the major steps manually, you should look at various software programs available for project portfolio management. Let us take a closer look at the software that is available.

Software Is Not Rocket Science

When considering the software that is available for use in project management today, it is helpful to first identify the various types of applications for software. They can be grouped into four basic types:

- **Project Management Software (PM):** This is defined as software that contains the tools to help a project manager execute a project, including scheduling, cost and budget controls, resource and task management, communication tools, charts and graphs to describe the project, and various measurement and documentation tools. Some project management software is designed for more simple projects, and others are for complex or multiple project events.

- **Collaborative Software (C):** This type of software allows people to collaborate on the same projects by using local or remote networks. Collaborative software is sometimes called groupware or social software. Examples include e-mail, videoconferencing, instant messaging, and chat.

- **Issue Tracking System (IT):** This software is deployed as an issue tracking system (sometimes called a trouble ticket or incident system) that maintains and manages issues relative to a project. An issue tracking system is similar to a bug tracker system, and often a software company will integrate an issue tracking system with a project management program.

- **Project Portfolio Management (PPM):** PPM is the process of managing the continuous flow of projects from concept to completion. This type of software is considered the next generation of project management software. Its model is borrowed from the financial world because it amalgamates all resources with their associated costs and compares that to the cost of lost business by not doing the project. This type of project management is used on mid to larger-sized companies or complex projects. Its objectives affect the business at a financial level, such as increasing shareholder value.

These four types of software will cover most projects, and there are thousands of them to choose from. For this work, we will focus on the more well known; however, the References section contains numerous Web sites where you will find other software programs that are available.

Of the four, collaborative software is the most widely known, as it includes such common platforms as e-mail, blog sites, instant messaging, and chat rooms. Most people today are familiar with these types of tools, but we will touch on them briefly in the context of effectiveness and protocols.

The use of technology or advanced software does not equate to success. You need to assess your own style, comfort level, and the needs of your organization. Although software can be extremely helpful, it is not necessarily required. Christina Majeed has managed projects successfully for two years without using any kind of project management software. She relies mostly on Excel spreadsheets.

CASE STUDY: CHRISTINA MAJEED

"I do not think the most important thing in managing a project is using the latest project management technology. Plus, not everyone on the team will know how to use all the latest technology.

I find Excel workbooks serve me well. It is easy, and my team members can go in and add to it. We are a computer software company, so I use a combination of our own internal system that we sell and use internally. This works well for me. To be an effective leader, having good communication and organization buys a lot more than inputting our data into a program. I like to work face to face or on the phone. I like to keep it focused."

As we spoke with project managers across the nation, we found that most of them use at least one element of industry-specific software. Microsoft Project was the software of choice, in particular, for the scheduling feature. For others, there were cost issues involved; purchasing several copies of proprietary desktop software, such as Microsoft Project, can become pricey if your company has many locations.

Joseph Zubay commented about the use of software in his capacity as a consultant of how to execute the most effective projects. He stresses that often, people are more concerned with fancy software than with knowing the business they are in. As a consultant, he needs to regularly step in and understand his client's business. He is surprised to learn how others do not seek that same level of knowledge.

CASE STUDY: JOSEPH ZUBAY

"The new project manager needs to understand the enterprise he is working in. If he is doing a project management job for a telecommunications company who is acquiring another company, he had best understand both companies before he begins. He needs to learn the organization, interview key people, and learn both businesses. The ability to do that rapidly will be quite beneficial. A new project manager's time is better spent on these kinds of activities than learning advanced software.

"In our business, almost everything that we do uses something as basic as Excel. Sometimes we use the database system too, but usually Excel. Sometimes we need to help a client go a little further, so we will go toward Project. We try to show them what they need to move something forward with the software. We do not recommend or train on software technology, but I think they all pretty much work the same from the very first systems that were developed in the late 1970s. They involve an action, an interval, and a value."

The final component to address is software that does not directly apply to project management but is important in day-to-day office operations. This group includes Microsoft Office products or the Apple iWork package, as well as bookkeeping and other common software in use today.

Integrated Project Management Software

Project Management Technology. The following list contains various software systems that are available for project management, from the most basic to the more advanced.

1. Open-Source Desktop Applications.

   Open-source desktop applications refer to computer software programs available under a license or on the public domain for use. These applications are acquired free via download.

One widely known example of an open-source desktop Web browser is Mozilla Firefox, which runs on Windows, Mac, and Linux. Firefox requires that you download it before using it.

Project Management software programs that are available as open-source desktop applications include:

a. Gantt Project (PM)

 1. Web site: **http://ganttproject.biz**

 2. Function: This is a free program that managers can use to generate Gantt charts. A project scheduling and management tool is included. Additional features include task hierarchy and dependencies, resource loading chart, PERT chart, reports in both PDF and HTML formats, and capability to import and export into Microsoft Project.

b. KPlato (PM)

 1. Web site: **www.koffice.org**

 2. Function: Project management program designed to help plan and schedule projects. Built-in features include Gantt charts with task land resource allocation list, task allocations per resource, and accounts view with costing identified by task. Built-in charts include Work Breakdown Structure (WBS), Resource Breakdown Structure (RBS), and Cost Breakdown Structure (CBS). Resource leveling is not included.

c. Open Workbench (PM)

1. Web site: **www.openworkbench.org**

2. Function: Windows-based project management software providing functionality of scheduling and managing projects. Includes WBS, RBS, and CBS. Program will show interdependencies, lag, and lead time. Scheduling option is automatic or manual and will cross master and subprojects. Other features include resource management and evaluation tools, such as PERT charts.

  d. TaskJuggler (PM)

1. Web site: **www.taskjuggler.org**

2. Function: Project management software primarily developed for Linux and Unix-like systems but now compatible with Windows and Mac operating systems. TaskJuggler provides functionality throughout the scope, resource assignment, cost and revenue planning, and risk assessment. It contains communication tools and its own built-in templates. It allows reports to be exported into both HTML and XML formats.

2. Open-source Web-Based Applications

Open-source Web-based applications refer to programs available under a license or on the public domain for use. These applications are Web-based and do not have to be downloaded to your desktop. Examples of open-source Web-based Web browsers are Ask, Google, or Yahoo!.

Project management software applications that are available as open-source Web-based applications include:

a. ProjectPier (PM) (C)

1. Web site: **www.projectpier.org**

2. Function: ProjectPier is a server-based project management/online collaboration application for the use of project managers across the world. This program is available in more than 17 languages. ProjectPier provides a platform for project managers to enter and track one or several projects. It is particularly strong at task management. However, it does not offer a forum for discussions among users, as do other project management platforms. Instead, ProjectPier publishes messages on your Web site and sends to users you specify via e-mail.

b. Bugzilla (IT)

1. Web site: **www.bugzilla.org**

2. Function: Bugzilla is server software intended to manage software development. This is not project management software; however, it is often used by project managers working on software deployment. It will catch "bugs" in your work and help you deliver a clean product.

c. dotProject (PM) (IT)

1. Web site: **www.dotproject.org**

2. Function: Free project management tool that also offers some issue-tracking features. dotProject's package includes user management, e-mail based trouble

ticket systems, unlimited project listings, hierarchical task lists, scheduling capacity, and discussion forums. dotProject also offers training that can either be purchased by non-members or accessed for free by members.

d. Project.net (PM) (C) (PPM) (IT)

1. Web site: **www.project.net**

2. Function: **Project.net** is a Web-based project management tool designed for dispersed teams within mid to large-sized companies. It is tailored for multiple projects. This program is rich with graphic tools and interactive capabilities. **Project.net** offers client services to help managers implement a project or install and configure to the manager's specifications. The company will also deliver training upon request. The product comes with access to online forums and contains issue-tracking features as well.

3. Proprietary Desktop Applications

Proprietary desktop applications are software programs available for purchase and installation onto a desktop. These programs may be licensed for either an individual or a company. Any time you go to a computer store and purchase software that you load onto your desktop, you are using a proprietary desktop application. There are many examples, such as Microsoft XP Operating System or Apple Mac Operating System. These software programs are not free and are licensed to one user, be it an individual or a company.

Project management software products that are available as proprietary desktop applications include:

a.   Artemis

1. Web site: **www.aisc.com**

2. Function: Several options of software applications are available, including product development, program management, IT management, and project management. Artemis has been producing products for more than 30 years, and as such, its scope of products is extensive. It also offers consulting, training, and other support.

b.   Microsoft Project (PM)

1. Web site: **www.msproject.com**

2. Function: A widely used program of project management, this software contains tools designed to control project work, schedules, and finances; keep project teams aligned; and be more productive through integration with familiar Microsoft Office system programs. There are also reports, graphs, and planning tools built into the software.

c.   Merlin (PM) (IT)

1. Web site: **www.merlin2.net**

2. Function: Project management software created to interface with Apple's Mac operating system. There are four different views that the project manager can use to assess the way the project is performing. The activities view is where the project is put together and the Gantt chart is generated. The Netplan view displays the critical path and the relationship between activities.

The utilization view shows which person is working on which task and if he or she is under or overused. Finally, the resource view allows you to manage and organize all the resources contained in the project.

d. OmniPlan

1. Web site: **www.omnigroup.com**

2. Function: Project management software created to interface with Apple's Mac operating system. This program is best used for simple or single projects, since it does not allow for file linkage or subprojects. Features include Gantt charts, schedules, summaries, milestones, and critical paths.

e. Sophocles (PM)

1. Web site: **www.sophocles.net/beta**

2. Function: Project management software for the writing industry, with particular focus on screenwriting. Still in the beta phase as of this writing, the company's Web site states that Sophocles 2007 will provide integrated screenwriting, story creation, scheduling, budgeting, and reporting functionality, all in a single, Windows-based desktop application. The three editions will be Basic, Professional, and PM. The Basic edition will comprise the core screenplay word-processing engine; the Professional edition will introduce advanced story-creation and analysis tools; and the PM edition will include the budgeting, scheduling, and reporting components.

4. Proprietary Web-Based Applications

Proprietary Web-Based Applications (sometimes called closed-source or non-free software) is software with restrictions on using it. These are programs that are accessed on the Web but require some sort of license agreement or contract with the user to access them. These platforms are used in a business-to-business environment where a client might need to log on to a proprietary Web site as part of his or her need to complete a business task. As a consumer, most people have used a proprietary Web-based application when ordering a product. An example of this type of application can be something like the Linden's Cookies Web site where consumers can order sweets, or something much bigger, such as Qwest Control™, which provides a broad range of communication services, such as dedicated hosting of Web sites, managed firewall, and more.

Project management software products that are available as proprietary Web-based applications include:

a. @task (PM) (C) (PPM) (IT)

1. Web site: **www.attask.com**

2. Function: Project management software with built-in support. Monthly subscription provides access to project management structure, a forum to get questions answered, and a client services number to get one-on-one assistance. The structure is comprehensive, from task lists to complicated charts. For a review of this company, see the article from *Information Week* dated March 13, 2006, by Roger Beall, which can be located at this address, **www.informationweek.com**, and searching for "attask."

b. Basecamp (C)

1. Web site: **www.basecamphq.com**

2. Function: A Web-based project management platform providing to-do lists, Writeboards (Web-based text documents), milestone management, messaging system, file sharing, and time tracking. There is much feedback about this company, managed by 37 Signals, because it is popular and widely used. The Web site says that more than a million people have signed up for Basecamp, for instance. However, there is some criticism that because it is trying to reach so many, there is little offered by way of custom or complex requirements. It does not offer Gantt charts, for instance.

c. Foldera (PM) (C) (PPM) (IT)

1. Web site: **www.foldera.com**

2. Function: A free filing system of Web-based folders used to organize and collaborate your project's work. This program can be used with multiple files and many people. Features include activity folders to organize your teams, projects, and information; file sharing with secure storage; e-mail sorted by project; task manager with assignment tracking; a contact manager to use for storing organizational information, calendar manager for scheduling, and more.

d. JIRA (IT)

1. Web site: **www.atlassian.com/software/jira**

2. Function: A Web-based program to identify and resolve "bugs." Additional features include generating built-in reports, help desk tickets and issues, built-in search engine, workflow mapping, and more. There is a feature tour on the Web as well as a demo you can download. Actual costs vary, depending on level of service purchased.

Software: Types

1. Microsoft Word, Excel, PowerPoint, Access, and Outlook

2. Apple Numbers, Pages, and Keynote

3. Intuit QuickBooks and Microsoft Money

4. Web-based conferencing

Microsoft Office is a product that contains three software programs: Word for word-processing documents; Excel for spreadsheet applications; and Outlook for e-mail, contacts, and calendar applications. Many people are familiar with the trio because it is widely used in corporations across the world. Thus, it is not uncommon to find project managers sending Excel spreadsheets all over the place, as attachments in e-mail. This book was typed in Word, and many of the spreadsheets that you find within it are imported from Excel. Beyond Office, other programs include Access, an advanced database program for large files to be sorted and compared, and finally, PowerPoint, slideshow presentation software that includes graphic art and animation as part of its package.

Likewise, Apple offers its own package of similar products, packaged as iWork. Like Office, iWork contains three programs that are built for the Mac: Pages is for word processing, Keynote is designed for presentations and includes animations and voice-over narration, and Numbers is a spreadsheet program.

Intuit produces both Quicken and QuickBooks, which are desktop software applications for tracking expenses. Quicken is targeted for personal use, such as maintaining household expenses, whereas QuickBooks is targeted for industry. QuickBooks is thought to be used by many accountants and business owners not only to track business expenses, pay bills, and manage taxes, but also to maintain a budget. Therefore, some project managers use this product to load and track their expenses and to stay on budget.

One alternative to the Intuit packages is Microsoft Money. This product is available in four different levels, from the basic package, Money Essentials, to Money Plus Home & Business, a package designed expressly for business.

It bears noting that many project management software programs also have cost and budget features built in. Microsoft Project, for instance, allows the user to enter costs and track them against a predetermined budget.

Remote Meeting Tools. In today's work environment, many project managers are responsible for managing a team across a geographic region. In the past, communication tools such as telephone, fax, or more recently, e-mail, were used to keep remote team members abreast of action items. Today, more companies are making use of video or Web-based conferencing.

This type of application is more commonly referred to as "Webinar" software and is growing increasingly popular as people seek an effective means to communicate with others across a geographic area. There are multiple choices of Webinar software today. You should research the various options available and schedule a call with the company's representative for the ones you find most appealing. The company's agent will explain any further requirements.

Effectively Using the Internet, Voice Mail, and Software

Voice Mail

We have not addressed voice mail with much detail in this work. The assumption is that most people know how to use it. Still, there are several rules you should follow for maximum effectiveness.

1. **Keep it brief**, less than 45 seconds. People do not like listening to long, rambling voice messages. Save the details for the live call.

2. **Always include your phone number**, even if you are certain everyone has it. You cannot assume that a person will be at his or her desk when the message is retrieved, so always leave the number to increase your chances for a quick return call.

3. **Your message may be forwarded or played for someone else.** Never leave anything on voice mail that you would not want shared with others, even if you mark it as private.

4. **If you are copying others in your voice message, say it at the onset of your message.** For instance, 'This is Barbara with a message to Joe, copying the team. I wanted you to know that I completed my aspect of the workbook and you can begin photocopying it whenever you are able.'

5. **Say when you wish a call to be returned, if appropriate.** Do not assume that the person you are calling will know you have a need to speak to him or her today.

E-mail.

1. **Reply to all e-mails within 24 hours**, even if it is a short acknowledgement that you have it and will give a more thorough reply in a day or two.

2. **When composing e-mails, use the To: box to address the message to the person whom you expect will take action upon the content**, the CC: box to copy any people who have a need to know about the message, and the BCC: box to anyone whom you want to share the message with, quietly. For example, suppose your boss has asked you to be more effective in your e-mails. You may wish to blind copy her (BCC) on key messages that you send so that she can evaluate your effectiveness. She is not part of the action item or a person who needs to be consulted, so there is no need for the rest of the team to realize that you blind-copied her. You use BCC when you need to copy someone privately.

3. **Your message might be forwarded or copied to others.** Even if you place a privacy status on your message, which prevents the message from being forwarded, that will not stop someone from copying and pasting it into a new message or printing it and sending it out in other ways. Never put anything into an e-mail message that you would not want to be shared with others outside the message.

4. **Use attachments to send documents.** Do not try to copy and paste Excel spreadsheets, for instance. Attach them instead.

5. **If you are sending something to others that is of a casual nature — a joke, for instance — use the BCC function for**

all the recipients, and do not forward as an attachment.
In an effort to reduce spam, you never want to forward your
associates' e-mail addresses randomly. Always protect their
privacy by using the BCC function, which does not pass
along their e-mail addresses. Be sure to not forward as an
attachment, however, because attachments will carry the e-
mail addresses of all involved.

There are other rules for voice mail and e-mail that you might wish to
employ in your particular situations. Let your company tell you specifics.
For now, the rules here should keep you at your most effective.

Chapter 12

Aliens Among Us?

This final chapter will address the benefits of joining a project management group and discuss whether the time required is something you should invest in.

About 35 percent of the project managers whom we spoke to said they are not currently active in a formal organization. They volunteered personal reasons as their primary reasons for not participating. Some of them were so overwhelmed by the demands of the day that the idea of taking on any more was not feasible, now. Others were going to school, and their schedules conflicted with the group's meeting dates.

Another 18 percent of our panel said they did not belong to any kind of formal organization; however, they did have associates who were also project managers. They meet with each other regularly to compare ideas, discuss new management tools, and vent at how frustrating things can become. Then, refreshed and armed with new information about the business, they return to their jobs, happier in the knowledge that they are not alone.

The remaining 47 percent of the group were members of some kind of association. The two that came up more than any others were PMI and **ProjectConnections.com**. However, there are many Web sites dedicated to project management. There are hundreds of chat rooms about it, too.

Let us take a step back and recall key advice that came up repeatedly from the project managers we interviewed. Many of them talked about the importance of communication, how a project's success depends on it and the importance of asking questions. You must obtain clarification about your deliverable. You must ask why and challenge if you are unsure or probe if you think your sponsor is unsure.

You are a new manager and new to project managing. You will have many questions. If your confidence levels are high, you will have no issue with asking multiple questions of your sponsor, manager, team members, or whomever you need help from.

As a typical manager newly promoted into an unfamiliar job, you know that you are eventually going to master the learning curve. Still, emotionally, there are many feelings of inadequacy, of wanting to prove yourself, even of wondering whether the job is the wrong match after all. Chances are good that you will find yourself in a situation where you need to find out how to do things, but you may be reluctant to ask as many questions as you should.

Find other project managers to mentor you. You can find them at the meetings, on the Web site, or in your own company but at another location. There are four good reasons to get into a project management organization as soon as possible, especially in your first couple of years:

Benefit #1: You will have other people to ask questions of without being perceived as unqualified for your job at your workplace.

Even beyond having a resource of other people to tap into when you have questions, members of a professional group will also have different experiences than you. The wisdom in a collective group outshines the wisdom of one person, no matter the industry. Sit in a room full of project managers and chances are good that you will learn something new, every time — a tip or a tool that will help you become more effective.

Benefit #2: You will learn about the latest tools that others are using. You will collect wisdom from the collective group, just by being there, which will enhance your own effectiveness.

Because project management is a discipline used across an array of industries, you will pick up information about other disciplines. You will have the opportunity to hear how project management is used in different industries, and it may trigger an idea or a career change.

Benefit #3: You will be networking with an array of people across multiple industries, allowing for learning, possible career changes, or friendships to occur.

Many of these organizations offer formal training or certifications. You can attend regular workshops to practice new skills or pursue a certification of your own.

Benefit #4: Education via workshops is available regularly. Certification is also offered regularly, allowing you to increase your personal value or negotiate for a raise.

CASE STUDY: BOB ECKERT

When we spoke with Bob Eckert, he was able to give us much detail about PMI. He is very active in the Minnesota Chapter of PMI and had this to say:

"There are local chapters, across the country and the world Minnesota happens to be one of the largest in with over 3,000 members. Our Web site is www. pmi-mn.org.

There are great things about the local chapter – you can network with other project managers across several industries, health care, construction, financial services – people from all disciplines are part of PMI MN. We have local interest groups, broken down by industries, too. We have round table sessions for an hour to talk about the issues in the industry. There is a networking group where, if you are a member, you can have access to your job posting board. Presentations

CASE STUDY: BOB ECKERT

relative to career networking on resume writing or interviewing skills are available. We have many volunteer speakers from all different areas come to talk. They address things such as Soft skills, disciplines, budgeting, and the like.

"Of course, there is certification training for project management. However the education extends to so much more."

CASE STUDY: KAREN THOMAS

Karen Thomas recommends **http:// ProjectConnections.com**.

"I use ProjectConnections. It is Web based, so I can get it anytime; I do not have to wait for a meeting. It has tons of resources — many of them are free, too. White papers, discussions, templates, case studies and interviews. I highly recommend the new project manager to get herself hooked into it now. It costs something like $20 a month or so, but it is well worth it."

We have offered you many reasons to link up with a professional project management organization, but here is the last one. Taking project management into the stratosphere will put you elbow to elbow with some real alien concepts, at first. It is good to know that you have friends out there. They can help you stay your course, sort through the minutia, and find the truth.

Conclusion

This book was devoted to assisting newly promoted managers and their team assistants gain comfort with the basic skills of project management. The variety of topics covered was robust. Our overarching goal was to offer you a sound platform of information, examples, and tools about the key concepts behind project management and the experience of managing a project so you could begin to develop your professional skills.

Toward that aim, we introduced you to the concepts and styles of management organizations, such as matrix and functional, so that you can recognize various structures used in business today. We explored some of the various managerial styles, such as by objectives or by walking around, so you are aware of different ways to manage a team. We provided an overview of the various ways to interact with your team, get to know them, learn to delegate, provide performance assessments and encourage them to stretch their skills. We contrasted the roles of manager and project manager in terms of the skills and criteria required for optimal success in either.

We then stepped through a simulated project from start to finish, explaining about phases and how they differ by industry. We demonstrated how the processes that initiate, plan, execute, control, and close apply to each phase as you move along on your project, no matter the industry. We explained need and feasibility studies, the project charter, deliverables, scheduling, activity lists, cost and budget estimating, risk and quality management, change requests, and managing variances. We introduced widely used formulas such as EVP and backward and forward pass. We created graphs reflecting our simulated project, such as the EVM, PERT, activities list, and resource allocation. We even included custom-made worksheets that our interviewees provided. We addressed when to abandon a project and what to expect from your team in that event.

We walked you through the intense planning stage and stressed the importance of careful execution and painstaking control. We created change to the project by having the sponsor add another deliverable to it, nearly at the end, so you could see how to respond. We provided the instructions about how to close down a project.

But the book's overarching goal is to provide enough detail so you can start to use the skills right away. So we went through multiple project skills, software options, and a brief word about the benefit of joining an organization.

The reason we are itemizing this is because we want to emphasize that there is much more out there to learn. Do not stop with this book. Research, join clubs, chat online, and read more books. Start a library right in your office and circulate books and articles to read among your team.

Your goal should be to seek more knowledge to gain more effectiveness in your work. You will want to master your learning curve as early as possible for two main reasons. First, because it will make doing your daily work easier and give it more impact; second, you will want to discover if you do not like this work, as early in the game as you can.

It could be that this position is one that you would just as soon move out of or, like some of the project managers we interviewed, you might put down roots and stick around for 15 or 20 years. You will not know until you gain proficiency and experience the thrill of a win a few times. If you do not like it, move on as soon as is professional and possible.

If you do like it, however, do not stop seeking ways to grow your knowledge.

There are appendices following this chapter. We believe you will find Appendix A particularly interesting; we detail the full responses that the project managers provided when asked these questions:

1. What are the areas that many new project managers find most difficult to overcome? Where do you see people struggling the most, and have you found any means around that?

2. What are the top reasons that you believe projects/project managers succeed or fail?

Appendix B highlights three Project Studies that our project managers submitted to us for publication. You can read through them — they are brief — and consider what made these Project Studies unique to the project manager and how each approached the problem.

You will also find a glossary that defines the more common project management terms.

Finally, at the end of this work is a reference and suggested reading list. This list also contains Web sites you can visit to evaluate project management and some Web sites that are specific to project management software.

We hope you found the information in this work helpful and adequate as you begin your new position. We wish you the best of success as you manage people and projects as part of your new role. Keep a positive attitude at the forefront of every day. It will come back to you.

Top Reasons Project Managers Succeed or Fail

This section contains quotes from the project managers interviewed for this work. We wanted to find out what they believed were the primary reasons that project managers succeed or fail. We asked them what areas they thought new project managers found most difficult to overcome — where they were struggling — then we asked them for their recommendations to overcome these challenges.

Many of our interviewees had similar answers. Following is a summary of what they said:

CASE STUDY: BOB ECKERT

"The key to success is to have a clear understanding of the requirements from the sponsor and the stakeholders, exercise excellent planning, and manage issues and risks. Failure stems from a lack of requirements, poor sponsorship, and poor project management skills.

"I think most new project managers do not know how to break a project down. I also see them struggling with budgeting and forecasting, developing WBSs, and understanding what the requirements are. Even seasoned project managers need to work at this. It is easy to say you have all the requirements, but if you do not, you stand the chance of rework, which is costly. Budgeting is important — I work closely with our finance people to ensure I am giving them the information they need."

CASE STUDY: MIKE HEUTMAKER

"Tasks that are fun will always get done — everyone likes working on fun projects and stuff they enjoy doing. Keep the team's spirit up, and you are more likely to succeed. Tasks fail for a number of reasons, but starting a meeting with 'Okay, here we go again with this project that everyone hates…' will breed this type of attitude. If your team sees that you do not care, they most likely will not either.

"I see project managers struggling with schedules and maintaining deliverables on schedule. The best thing I have found is to know your team very well. You learn very quickly who typically meets their commitments and who does not. This applies to the manager and subordinate levels with your teams. I have always liked to rely on managers to provide updates and keep their people on task. The manager should know what his/her direct reports are working on and whether they are making their scheduled commitments — and if not, why not."

CASE STUDY: SARY MABJISH

"First, for the project to succeed, you have to have the support of upper management. Senior management has to agree about how we proceed with the budget and the time line, for instance. Without that, everything you do will fail. Second, you also must have the commitment of the team members. The team members were chosen for a reason, and they are the ones who will do the work. It is important that they are committed and will do the action items, no matter how often we meet.

"I think one of the things that new project managers have trouble with is motivating people. This ties back to selecting your team members. If you can select them, that is one thing, but other times, they are given to you. Sometimes, team members have a project to do in addition to their daily work. They are not always fully motivated to do the project. New project managers will need to discuss the project and time lines and also to motivate team members. It is important to encourage them to see the big picture and use techniques to help.

"While it is not our job to do the actual (task) work, sometimes you have to initiate the work for the team members to get motivated. This worked in my case. We

CASE STUDY: SARY MABJISH

had to write a big document, and the team was not excited to start. I kept talking to them about seeing the big picture, but it was not working. I got the project started by starting the document myself and giving it to them to continue. I motivated them by starting it and showing them how — that it was attainable."

CASE STUDY: DAN MASON

"If you do your homework and plan right, you will see the pitfalls and succeed. If sponsors put too much responsibility on you, you cannot decide for them, because you do not have the authority. Everyone has to be on the same page. That is what I love about Microsoft Project — you can see what tasks are dependent on others. Failure can also occur when the project manager is afraid to tell key people the truth. Let the systems do it for you, until you are able to do it yourself. Somebody has to.

"I see many new project managers who are also new to management. They have some difficulty taking an authoritative role. They wish everyone would keep to their commitment and schedules and do not want to have to correct anyone. It took me about a year to realize that I will never fire anyone from a project or a job. They will fire themselves. Because as an effective manager, I will first communicate what I expect from everyone, then correct them when they are not performing at the levels they need to be, then warn them if it is repeated, then let them go. This kind of expectation is fair to them and sends a message to the rest of the team. I cannot be responsible for the behavior of everyone on my team, but I am responsible for communicating their expectations. I am also responsible for asking them what they need, if they are not performing. If I get them everything they need and they still do not perform, it is time to let them go."

CASE STUDY: CHRISTINA MAJEED

"As for the biggest reasons they succeed or fail, my answer is the same — leadership. I think things fail because of poor leadership and succeed if they have been led well. A good leader will not place blame or fault their team for a project's failure but will take ownership of the issues and employ creativity in turning failures into successes.

CASE STUDY: CHRISTINA MAJEED

"Time is the biggest challenge. I think the reason why some project managers struggle with it is because they try to be too organized; they try to be perfect. During my day, I have a list of things I want to accomplish. I map them out, i.e., before lunch and after lunch. In project management, so many things pop up that you cannot anticipate. It is difficult to find time to fix those issues when you are too rigid in your schedule. I try to be as flexible as possible. I have a list taped to my desk every week of what needs to be done in each project, by Friday. When I put together my schedule, I leave room for the unforeseeable. If nothing unforeseeable arises, I keep working the list to get ahead."

CASE STUDY: PEGGY SANCHEZ

"Success is related to the attitude of key people. We had a project handed to us that had to be completed in two weeks, and it was done entirely by attitude. We kept saying, 'Wow. We got this done.' It created momentum. People started to pick up slack for others. If you are going to have a meeting and there are supposed to be ten people and someone is not there, someone else at the meeting will pick up the phone and do things outside of their job to get it done, if they believe in it.

"Project managers fail when there is no accountability for missing deadlines. If we miss a date and people begin to make excuses, it is important for the project manager to step in. Even if there are problems, the project must get done. Hold the team accountable for milestones.

"I see project managers struggling to know how much they need to understand. In my business, you do not have to understand the technical side to get something done. If I understand who the experts are, then I do not have to understand the technical part as much as what the goal is. Project managers should focus on the deliverable as opposed to the technical side. If you get drawn into the business itself, you will lose sight of your own goals.

"Another big item for new project managers is to realize they have the onus. For me, I realized early on that I have as much authority as I want. I am responsible for making others accountable. I can tell them if they are having a problem, then I will need to escalate so that they can make my item a priority. You do not do this as a threat — you do it to facilitate their priorities. If their respective managers tell them to do something before my project item, they cannot decide to do

CASE STUDY: PEGGY SANCHEZ

otherwise. So, I go escalate when I need to. I have had to tell managers above me that if they are not going to be able to do this, I will have to escalate to see what we can do. If I cannot get the resource, I will go to my boss and let him make that call. It is best to take the authority to step in.

"It is about confidence. Anytime I hedge on something, people will tell me that we cannot do that, but if I say yes, we are going to do it and stop complaining, it is amazing how much people will respond."

CASE STUDY: PAUL SCHOEN

"One of the top reasons projects succeed or fail is the project managers themselves. Ultimately, if your team is failing or you cannot deliver, it is your job to manage that risk and notify people. If it is beyond your control, you need to engage others to help you. Failing to plan, failing to budget properly, and creating schedules that are too tight also contributes to failure. If you miss a deadline, your project should not fail. It usually means the project manager did not plan enough.

"It is also essential that new project managers learn not to take things personally and that they consider the feelings of team members as well. Do not chastise your team in a public meeting if someone misses a day. Also, build buffer into the schedule, as much as you can, to allow for lateness. Protect yourself. People can be competitive — do not be afraid to tell your boss your project is failing, but do not do it at the end, when you cannot recover. Give a status report every two weeks or so to your boss and sponsor, whether it is required or not. That helps them to share in the responsibility."

CASE STUDY: KAREN THOMAS

"One of the reasons projects fail is lack of communication. I pull my team together every single day. I get a lot of grief from other project managers about that, but I view it like a sales status meeting. When I was in sales, I used to have to report to my manager every day about how many prospects I had, then I would go sell.

CASE STUDY: KAREN THOMAS

"It pumped me up. In project management, I do the same thing with my team. I use those morning meetings to get people awake and ready to work, instead of letting them wake up slowly, at their desks, over coffee while reading e-mail. When we finish those meetings, everyone is awake and we all know exactly who is going to do what, and why, that day. As for the sponsors, I status them via e-mail every Friday morning in a semi-casual manner, then I follow up with a phone call to ask if we can talk over certain items. Many times, we do it by phone, but for complicated things, I go over to their building. We usually have a meeting once a week. I am more relaxed about these things because I have been doing it for almost 20 years. I like project management and have no desire to move out of it. I know the craft, I know my sponsors, and everything is cool. Communication is a requirement of the job. Do it every day, face to face, with your team, and they will have constant statuses, questions answered, and problems faced.

"New project managers struggle because they are not comfortable asking for help. As new project managers, they are uncertain what is most important. They are trying to learn the craft while running the project. I had that same challenge when I started out. I was promoted from sales into this, and all I knew about project management was what I saw others doing. I was afraid to say I needed help because I thought it would indicate they had made a mistake in promoting me. I tried to muck through it, and it did not work out well. If a new project manager is reluctant to ask questions of sponsors or managers, ask team members. If they have a problem with helping someone new, then at least join a group of project managers, like PMI. There are PMI chapters all over the country. You do not have to be certified to join. You can ask questions of those people, without any risk. You could also get online and join a Web-based group, or go out to Craigslist, if all else fails. There are discussion boards about project management all over the place. There is no excuse not to ask questions about the craft. If you have questions about the business that you are in, you will have to talk to your company. But get out there and learn what you need."

CASE STUDY: MIKE TULIPON

"I think projects have more success when everyone knows who is accountable. Failure comes when people do not have accountability for their actions. They hem and haw about not knowing they had to do things, they begin to doubt their own abilities, and it snowballs.

CASE STUDY: MIKE TULIPON

"So much can be avoided with accountability. I keep my people — and myself — accountable by using a tool on our company's Web site. Our company has a "back office" on its Web site, meaning when we go to the corporate Web site, there is a place where each retail store can log in to its own Web site, or where the admin people, like me, can log in to our own Web site. My team goes to my company.com/tulip and there is all our stuff. I keep files of every project there. Some are active and some are archived, but they are all there. The technology we use allows me to lock certain ones up, when I need to, or password protect areas of the project to prevent anyone from going in there and making changes. When changes are made, the software actually puts an indicator next to each line showing who made the change, similar to Microsoft Word's way of tracking changes in a document. So, when we log in to the Tulip room, we all see the same thing, in real time. If I go in right now and make an update to an activity, all my team will see it update instantly. Likewise when others make changes. It is very effective.

"I make this Web site accessible to my sponsor and other stakeholders so they can go in at any time and see the status, too, but I still do the progress reports and meet with them when I need to. I cannot depend on them going in to check the status. I bring them the issues and status them all the time. Everybody knows what is going on.

"New project managers struggle because they do not want to ask "why." You have to ask that question constantly. Every time they give you an answer, ask why again. You have to understand why you are doing things and what you are going to produce. They also struggle with the need to see both the big picture and all the details. This is hard, especially if the new project manager does not fully understand their industry. You might have 20 years experience doing project management in a retail world, like me, but put me into an environment like NASA, where everyone talks in acronyms and I know nothing about the technology — it would take adjusting. You must rely on the strengths you have during times like that and show confidence. Ask questions and you will be fine."

CASE STUDY: BINH VO

"If the project is successful, it is a team effort. If it fails, it is the fault of the project manager. I stress that there is only a certain personality type that should go into project management. You need thick skin — the ability to take on failures and learn from them.

CASE STUDY: BINH VO

"Balance is key. Teams change — you have to balance them. Variances occur — you have to balance them, usually by communication. Communicate constantly. Team performance fluctuates — you have to balance it. Give feedback right away if someone is producing less than what you need. There is a balance to being empathetic and giving feedback. Various functions are sometimes at odds — you have to balance them, by getting each person to focus on the project. In this case, you may need to use patience to allow things to balance on their own. You cannot force an analyst to immediately get along with the development team. You have to be patient to allow them to trust each other. Sometimes you can be the enabler, and sometimes you have to wait for things to occur."

CASE STUDY: JOSEPH ZUBAY

"Often, a project will be launched because somebody in a position of influence in a company gets what they believe is a good idea. They might prepare to implement this idea without knowing if it is a good idea. How would you know? Many say the way to find out if your idea is good is to put together a business case. So, they do that. But it is not objective — it is a proven business case. They begin, then they call us in to give them a hand. They are running into roadblocks because they did not really have it set. When you get the business case fixed to where it is accurate, it might turn out that it was not such a good idea. Do not implement without a business plan made by neutral parties. You cannot have the inventor of the idea as the same person who proves it to be a good idea. The smart manager will put together a team of neutral parties for this.

"New project managers struggle the most with communication. I was just working for a client who has a project manager doing a pretty good job keeping all the organizations tied together across huge distances and disciplines, but he is having difficulty with the people because they think he is a geek and an extremist. They see him as a perfectionist who is unreasonable with dates. This is the nature of project management, so what is he doing wrong? He needs to change his approach to be more facilitative. When he asks for a date, the person whom he asks needs to believe that giving him the date will benefit them. He needs to be more empathetic. Show benefits — do not lecture.

CASE STUDY: JOSEPH ZUBAY

"It is people skills. The project manager has to take the position that nobody is helping him get his job done; they are helping him get everybody's job done. If the project manager can be perceived as a facilitator of everyone he is working for, he will be more easily accepted. The project manager's bosses have to understand that too because they are usually the perpetrator of this kind of behavior. By not understanding, they can drive the project manager to become demanding. This is a learned set of behaviors. Communicate with empathy, and show people the benefits of why they need to help you."

Project Studies

The cases listed in this appendix are actual ones. They are provided to demonstrate some of the remarkable accomplishments of project managers. As you read them, you will see how the teams reacted to challenges. Take some tips from their actions.

PROJECT ONE: MIKE HEUTMAKER & HUMAN MAN INTERFACE

Mike Heutmaker has worked as a project manager for five years for Digi International out of Minneapolis, Minnesota. Prior to that, he was a project engineer for another eight years. He describes one project that was remarkable for a couple of reasons: first, because the deliverable was nearly impossible, and second, because he would leave the company as soon as it was completed. Here is the story, in his own words:

When did your project take place and what was the background?

I managed a project for Kontron Mobile Computing (KMC) in Minneapolis, Minnesota, from January through July of 2006. A bit of background: KMC was called Fieldworks when I started working there in 1996 as a project engineer. About 2000, Fieldworks was purchased by a German company named Kontron (**www.kontron.com**) and became Kontron Mobile Computing. Kontron acquired several companies in the United States and began consolidating operations to two facilities in California. I was offered a position in California but did not take it. I was given approximately eight-months notice that the offices in Minnesota were closing and that my last day with the company would be July 1, 2006. The office closed soon after this.

What were your deliverables?

PROJECT ONE: MIKE HEUTMAKER & HUMAN MAN INTERFACE

Deliverable was a replacement Human Man Interface (HMI) for an aging solution in all U.S. Budweiser breweries. Existing systems were nothing more than desktop computers built into stainless steel enclosures. The CRT display was viewable only through a glass window in this enclosure. Sealed keyboards were used to interface with this outdated solution. These systems needed to be able to be cleaned with a pressure washer and had to meet the FDA requirements for equipment on the brewery floor. These computers were used for controlling all functions related to brewing beer in very large quantities.

Our solution was a one-piece system that contained a large, bright LCD display that was "piggy backed" with a rugged computer. The brewery employees simply would remove the glass window they normally viewed their CRT display through and bolt in our solution (onto an existing hole pattern). The display also housed a sealed touch screen, eliminating the need for a separate keyboard. All brewing functions could now be controlled using simple touch commands on the screen. This solution could be sprayed with a pressure washer and would not allow any water to penetrate the enclosure.

Who were the team members?

As with many projects I have worked on in the past, resources were spread all over the globe. Hardware engineering was done in Freemont, California, first prototype systems were built in Poway, California, Software developed in Minnesota and with Budweiser team, and so on.

What made it challenging?

Several things. First, we were scheduled to deliver our first production units in June, and my last day with the company was July 1. The logistics of keeping everyone on track were also a challenge. Calls to and from Malaysia had to be made at 4:30-6 a.m. (CST), or after 6 p.m. Calls to California had to fit their schedules as well. This meant many early mornings and late nights trying to ensure everyone had what they needed and was on track. The customer was demanding and had its own release schedules for this project that it had made for its management teams. There were several schedules that needed to be considered any time a decision was made that might affect our schedule.

How did you resolve the challenge?

We set the team's expectations up front. We completed team buy-in on schedule before it was presented it to the customer. We held meetings twice a

PROJECT ONE: MIKE HEUTMAKER & HUMAN MAN INTERFACE

week with our engineering and Malaysian teams to coordinate the transfer of data and information. We had to coordinate having some long lead-time parts that our Malaysian production house could not get in time for our production build, run here in the U.S. and then sent to them to "shorten" their production lead times. Had we not done this, we could not have met our dates.

How did it turn out?

With the exception of a one-week delay in sending our first production units to the customer, we did maintain our schedules. We identified this delay a few weeks before the units were to ship and alerted the customer so they could make the needed adjustments to their plan. In the end, they were happy we identified the delay as soon as we knew about it. The systems are still shipping and are replacing the outdated systems they had been using. I left Kontron on July 1, 2006, and have heard reports that this project is meeting everyone's expectations and the systems continue to ship and work well.

PROJECT TWO: BOB ECKERT & DAYLIGHT SAVINGS TIME CHANGE

Bob Eckert, PMP, has led IT Infrastructure projects for more than 15 years and has been a Senior Systems Integrator for the last 9 years.

When did your project take place, and what was the background?

It was Tuesday, January 23, when I was assigned to be the Project Manager for the 2007 Daylight Savings Time Change. President Bush signed the Energy Act of 2005, and as a result, Daylight Savings Time would begin on Sunday, March 11 at 2:00 a.m. and would conclude on Sunday, November 3, at 2:00 a.m. Prior to the signing of this Act, Daylight Savings Time would have occurred on Sunday, April 1, and would have gone back to Standard time on October 28.

What were your deliverables?

Create a Project Charter and build a team of resources that spanned the enterprise, which included over 30 remote sites across the United States, three service providers, and several vendors, to determine what the potential impacts are, what systems are affected, what can be done to mitigate the impact, and who will be impacted. If there was a risk to our systems, we needed to understand

PROJECT TWO: BOB ECKERT & DAYLIGHT SAVINGS TIME CHANGE

what was required to fix it so they would be able to function after the time change. Our deliverables were due no later than March 1, 2007.

Who were the team members?

We had 80 point people who were located throughout the country, and they worked with our vendors to determine what the impacts were and what we could do to resolve those impacts. We also worked with three service providers that were responsible for the management of our data center, network, and desktops.

What made it challenging?

We had a firm delivery date and 36 calendar days to determine what the impacts were, what we could fix before March 1, and what risks we felt comfortable accepting. In addition, we had remote resources that were working with vendors, and we needed to synchronize the vendors' implementation schedules with the schedules we had to accommodate any changes to our systems. Throughout the project, we had customers asking for assurances that our systems would be ready and would not impact their systems after the time change. Any changes that had to be made to our homegrown applications had to go through our entire development life cycle, which is time consuming. We could not impact any service level agreements we had with internal or external customers. We assumed that the systems that had the largest potential for impacts were our Blackberry users, e-mail users, servers, and other infrastructure-related devices.

How did you resolve the challenge?

We broke the project down by area and assigned a point person to each area. I kept a master risk log, which included 333 risks that needed to be mitigated, and we determined an additional 41 that we accepted as low or no risk. Each point person assembled a team to determine which systems needed to be looked at and which systems required help from our service providers or vendors and began managing each risk. As the risks were mitigated, we closed them on the risk log and reviewed our progress at the weekly project status meeting.

How did it turn out?

We met our March 1 deliverable date. The time change occurred and was nearly seamless. We had one issue with one vendor that caused an outage to one of our internal teams. There were also a few desktops that had not been patched. Our external customers experienced no outages. Overall, the project was a success.

PROJECT THREE: CHRISTINA MAJEED & THE TRADE SHOW DASH

Christina Majeed has been the head of the electronic medical records (EMR) section at NexTech Corporation for the past two years. The EMR section is relatively new (four years in development) in the company, so everything to do with EMR comes to her desk, from suggestions from clients to how to incorporate company-driven changes into the software. She shares the following case study:

When did your project take place and what was the background?

The project took place in February of 2006. We were preparing our new Electronic Medical Records (EMR) software for an annual medical trade show. This trade show is one of the most important trade shows we attend throughout the year. Our presence at this trade show needed to make a positive impact, for this was just the second time we attended the show, and we wanted to establish ourselves as a strong presence in this market.

What were your deliverables?

Fully functional and smoothly working software for sales reps and the technical team to demo and sell to prospects at the trade show.

Who were the team members?

The team members were the project manager, various in-house software programmers, and trainers who had previous experience with our software and with the prospects we would be selling to at the trade show.

What made it challenging?

Time and working with people who were in different offices, specialties, and areas of the country.

How did you resolve the challenge?

We clearly mapped out the objectives and prioritized what was necessary to have at the trade show. In addition, we stayed organized and in communication throughout the project. Our team held meetings every morning to go over progress and project what could be accomplished that particular day. Focus, hard work, clear communication, and positive attitudes are what allowed us to accomplish our goal in a two-week time frame.

PROJECT THREE: CHRISTINA MAJEED & THE TRADE SHOW DASH

How did it turn out?

We achieved our goal of establishing our presence in that particular market and increased sales by 150 percent from the time we attended our first trade show in 2005 until this one, in 2006. Even better, our existing clients who received the software upgrade were extremely happy with the new version. It was a success.

Glossary

A

Accountability: Alignment of consequences to people based on their performance.

Action: A synonym for task.

Action Plan: A plan that describes what needs to be done and by when.

Activities Plan: A table that shows the planned activities and their associated start and end dates.

Activities Report: A table that lists project activities with their planned start and end dates against their actual start and end dates.

Activity: A unit of work, often broken down into tasks, that requires resources and time to complete.

Actual Cost (AC): Part of Earned Value Management (EVM), AC refers to the actual costs for the work done on an activity during a specified period.

Arc: The line connecting two nodes in a Program Evaluation and Review Technique (PERT) or critical path method (CPM) network.

Assumption: 1. Something presumed but not stated, often leading to a misunderstanding. 2. A rule that a project manager creates that can also be changed.

Audit: A formal and detailed examination of the progress, costs, operations, results, or some other aspect of a project or system.

Availability: The amount of time a person is actually on the job.

B

Background: The statement of condition explaining why a project was created, by whom, and identifying its main stakeholders.

Backing In: The process of identifying activities and duration estimates that equal the project's allotted time by starting at the end of a project and working backward.

Backward Pass: The process of calculating latest allowable start and finish dates for each activity by beginning at the end of a project and moving backward.

Bar Chart: See Gantt Chart.

Baseline: The plan that guides the costs, time schedule, and other variables in the project and is used to measure the performance of the activities in the project.

Benchmarking: Establishes a point of reference and set of standard metrics for measuring the success of a project or activities in a project.

Benefit Cost Analysis: A comparative assessment of a project's expected benefits compared to its estimated costs.

Budget: A detailed estimate of the costs of a project over a period.

C

Constraints: The restrictions that are imposed on the project that limit what the project must achieve, how, by when, and at what cost.

Contingency: An amount of time or money that is put aside to be used if risk events occur. Operates at the level of the whole project.

Contingency Plan: An alternative plan of action to be implemented if a risk event occurs.

Control: A process for comparing actual results with planned performance, analyzing the difference, and taking corrective action.

Cost Benefit Analysis: An analysis used to evaluate a proposed course of action.

Critical Activity: An activity or event that, if delayed, will delay an important event or the project itself.

Critical Path: The sequence of activities in a project that take the longest time to complete and thereby determines the minimum schedule for a project.

Critical Path Method (CPM): A means to determine project duration by reviewing the network diagram, finding the critical path, and calculating the schedule by estimating the earliest start and finish dates, then estimating the latest start and finish dates and using the difference between the two start dates and finish dates to compute the float for a task.

D

Delegation: Assigning some of your responsibilities to someone else.

Deliverable: The result of a project or task. Deliverables and output are synonymous. Deliverables can be organizational attributes, reports, and plans or physical products or objects.

Dependency Diagram: Another name for a network or precedence diagram that shows the relationship between two tasks, where one's start or finish is linked to another.

Duration: The actual calendar time that a task or project will take from start to finish and that you will use to develop the schedule for a project.

Duration Compression: Shortening the time required for a task or project by assigning additional resources to it.

E

Early Finish: Earliest time an activity may be finished. This calculation is identified when using the Forward Pass Calculation.

Early Start: Earliest time an activity may be started. This calculation is identified when using the Forward Pass Calculation.

Earned Value (EV): Part of Earned Value Management (EVM), EV refers to the budgeted amount for a particular activity, during a specified period.

Earned Value Management (EVM): A method to calculate and examine project performance by comparing the amount of work expected against actual accomplishments.

Effectiveness: A measure of the quality of attainment in the delivery of the desired results.

Effort: The amount of work or labor (in hours or workdays) that it takes to do a task or project, normally expressed in person-hours or person-days.

Escalation: The process of approaching a higher level of authority to communicate an issue and get help addressing a risk or problem.

Estimation: The art of developing a best guess about what costs and delivery dates will be.

Event: A significant occurrence that takes place at a specific point in time.

Exclusion: An item that will be omitted from the project.

Expectation: An item or output that a person wants as part of a delivery. Often not clearly defined.

F

Fast-Tracking: Performing two or more activities concurrently to reduce the project time.

Float: The amount of time a task can be delayed without affecting other tasks in a project. Also known as slack time.

Functional Management: The standard departments of a business organization that align with specialized disciplines, such as engineering, marketing, purchasing, and accounting.

G

Gantt Chart: A chart composed of bars on a schedule and other symbols to illustrate multiple time-based activities or projects on a horizontal time scale.

Gate: Another term for a milestone, with focus being on obtaining approval to pass through the gate.

Go/no-go Indicator: A level of measurement that reveals whether a deliverable is within predefined limits and whether a project or activity should be changed, terminated, or continued.

Grade: A ranking that compares two or more items that have the same functional use but do not share the same quality requirements.

H

Hierarchical Planning: A planning exercise in which each managerial level breaks tasks down into the activities that must be done at that level.

I

Imposed: Set by the customer, whether or not it is possible to accomplish in the project.

Inclusion: Something that will be included in the project.

Indirect Costs: Expenditures and items that support projects but are not tracked by the projects.

Infusion: A way of terminating a project by incorporating the project operations and team into the organization as part of the normal business operations.

Initiate: The progress that, when exercised, creates the beginning of a project or phase of a project, by demonstrating the need.

Iterate: To repeat continuously to achieve a higher quality output, greater accuracy, or finer detail.

L

Lag: The time delay between the start or finish of one activity and the start and finish of the next activity.

Late Finish: The latest time an activity may be finished and still remain within the confines of the schedule. This calculation is identified when using the Backward Pass Calculation.

Late Start: The latest time an activity may be started and still remain within the confines of the schedule This calculation is identified when using the Backward Pass Calculation.

Lead: A condition in which the start of one task occurs before the finish of its predecessor.

Leveling: The process of shifting the use of resources to even out the work load of team members and equipment during times of peaks and valleys.

Loading: The amount of time individual resources have committed to a project; refers to work load.

M

Make or Buy Analysis: A means to evaluate whether it is more effective to build something from scratch or to buy a standard product on the open market.

Matrix Organization: An organizational structure in which people from different parts of the organization work on a project and are managed by their functional supervisors and the project supervisors.

Milestone: A point in the project that marks the attainment of a goal or a set of tasks.

Mixed Organization: This organizational structure includes functional groups and pure project groups, similar to a matrix organization.

Model: A type of an example of reality, normally simplified for understanding the context.

Multi-Project Analysis: A method used to analyze the impact to activities when more than one project is underway and the progress of one group affects the other, especially as it relates to groups sharing people and equipment.

N

Negative Float: The state at which all the float in a project is spent and schedule dates will be impossible to meet, making the project come in late.

Network Diagram: A flow chart illustrating the sequence of work in a project.

O

Output: A synonym for deliverable.

P

Padding: A standard project management tactic used to add a little extra time or money as part of contingency planning or to avoid risk.

PERT: Acronym for Program Evaluation and Review Technique, describing a network diagram that employs three estimates (best, least, and most likely) to describe the range of an activity's span time.

Phase: A grouping of logically related activities that normally produce a deliverable.

Planned Value (PV): Used as part of Earned Value Management (EVM), PV defines the budget that was approved for a particular activity on the WBS, during a specified period.

Precedence: When a task cannot start until another ends, the ending task is said to have precedence.

Precedent: A precedent is something that must happen in order for the next task to happen. You cannot copy a document until you write it. The activity of writing it is a precedent to the activity of copying.

Pro Forma: Projected or anticipated, as in financial data found on balance sheets or income statements.

Process: A routine series of steps that comprise a function.

Product Development Life Cycle: A set of phases and steps to bring a product to market in an industry or company.

Production: Regular, routine work that is repeated continuously and produces the same products, services, or results time after time.

Project: A sequence of interrelated and interdependent tasks with a defined start and end date that use time and resources to produce a unique product, service, or other result.

Project Charter: The document issued by senior management that formally authorizes the project manager's authority to spend resources and time on a project and to direct project members.

Project Life Cycle: The time it takes to complete an entire project from the onset of the first task to the conclusion of the last task.

Project Management (PM): The application of knowledge, systems, techniques, tools, and people required to meet the project's requirements.

Project Management: A system used to diagram activities and data and Information Systems (PMIS) to track progress and information flow in a project.

Project Management Information Systems (PMIS): A system used to diagram activities and data and to track progress and information flow in a project.

Project Management Process: The five steps of initiating, planning, executing, controlling, and closing.

Project Manager: A person who is assigned and takes responsibility for defining the purposes and coordinating a project, regardless of size, to make sure the desired result comes in on time and within budget.

Project Plan: A set of documents that evolve over the first three project phases that guide all the work of the project.

Project Portfolio Management (PPM): PPM is the process of managing the continuous flow of projects from concept to completion. It is a group of projects together in a set, managed by one project manager.

Project Schedule: The schedule of project work on a calendar with each task's start and finish date populated.

Q

Quality: The traits of each project's deliverable that are predefined to meet the stakeholders' requirements.

Quality Assurance: The means to test the deliverables and their components before and during delivery to ensure the sponsor's specifications are met.

Quality Control: Refers to an ongoing quality management and review of the process of doing the work of the project.

Quality Management: The process required to ensure that a project will satisfy the needs for which it was deployed.

Quality Management Plan: The document that identifies quality standards specific to the project and the means to satisfy them.

R

Risk: Anything that decreases the chances that a project will achieve a desired result.

Risk Analysis: The process of assessing possible risks and their potential effects on a project and creating plans to minimize any negative effects.

S

Scope: A high-level description of everything to be included in and excluded from a project.

Scope Creep: The process of adding additional features or customers to the middle of a project, until the original schedule and cost estimates are meaningless.

Situational Management: The approach of matching management style to the specific needs of a situation.

Slack: See Float.

Stage: A set of related tasks leading to the completion of a major deliverable or milestone. Also called a phase.

Stakeholders: People or groups who are necessary to a project or who will be affected by the project.

Statement of Work: A document showing the integrated set of tasks, goals, risks, and assumptions that accompany the project plan during its development.

Subproject: A group of activities that comprise a project in their own right but are a part of the main project, such as planning to build a store within a mall while you plan the mall itself.

Subtask: A portion of the complete task. For instance, the task might be to tally sales results for a sales manager's entire group, and a subtask would be to pull a report for each sales person.

System Development Life Cycle: A series of stages used as a template to plan a project and increase the likelihood of project success.

Systems Approach: A wide-ranging approach to problem solving that considers multiple and interacting relationships. Project management is an example of a systems approach.

T

Task: A subactivity, a job that is too minor to be included in the first level of detail in a Work Breakdown Structure but is often included in the second level.

Termination Team: A project team responsible for closing down the administrative details of a project, sometimes referred to as executing the punch-out list.

Total Float: The cumulative time span in which the completion of all activities may occur and not offset the termination date of the entire project.

W

Webinar: A term referring to a "Web-based seminar" or teleconferencing.

Work Breakdown Structure (WBS): An organized, hierarchical diagram that lists all the work that must be done by each person to complete a project.

Work Package: The smallest unit of the Work Breakdown Structure.

References

Baker, Sunny and Kim and Campbell, G. Michael. *The Complete Idiot's Guide to Project Management, Third Edition.* New York: Penguin Group, 2003.

Beall, Roger. *Information Week.* Review: *Project Management Software.* March 13, 2006. CMP Media LLC, 2007. (**www.informationweek. com/news/showArticle.jhtml;jsessionid=KBJHWWHNDYF3IQS NDLPCKH0CJUNN2JVN?articleID=181502663&pgno=1&quer yText=**)

Belker, Loren B. and Topchik, Gary S. *The First-Time Manager, Fifth Edition.* New York: AMACOM, 2005.

Heerkens, Gary R. *Project Management.* New York: McGraw-Hill, 2002.

Kemp, Sid, PMP. *Project Management DeMystified.* New York: McGraw-Hill, 2004.

Lewis, James. P. *Fundamentals of Project Management, Third Edition.* New York: AMACOM, 2007.

Project Management Institute. *A Guide to the Project Management Body of Knowledge (PMBOK® Guide) Third Edition.* Pennsylvania: Project Management Institute, 2004.

Portnoy, Stanley E. *Project Management for Dummies, Second Edition.* New Jersey: Wiley Publishing, Inc., 2007.

Web References

The Association for Project Management. **www.apm.org.uk**

Big Dog's Bowl of Biscuits. Leadership resource site. **www.nwlink. com/~donclark**

Institute for Management Excellence. **www.itstime.com/oct96. htm#top**

NASA's EVM tutorial. **http://evm.nasa.gov/definition1a.html**

Project Management Institute. **www.pmi.org/Pages/default.aspx**

Rensselear Polytechnic Institute. **www.rpi.edu/dept/advising/free_ enterprise/business_structures/management_styles.htm**

Sciforma Corporation. (Web-based PM tools) **www.sciforma.com**

Spottydog Project Management Center. **www.spottydog.u-net.com**

Additional Links for Project Management Software

1. Product: 4 p.m.

   - Link: **www.4pm.com/articles/selpmsw.html**

   - Their Claim: In our five-step project methodology, we teach people to use project software so they can build schedules quickly and update them in minutes a week.

2. Product: Easyprojects.

- Link: **www.easyprojects.net**

- Their Claim: The easiest all-in-one Web-based project management software for project managers or their assistants.

3. Product: MinuteMan Systems.

- Link: **www.minuteman-systems.com**

- Their Claim: Our project management products are used in a wide variety of applications, including construction, engineering, office management, inventory control, and legal preparation. Use our products to track time, people, expenses, or simply to organize information.

4. Product: TWiki™.

- Link: **www.twiki.net/index.html**

- Their Claim: TWiki has been tested over nine years by a growing open-source community. Twiki is an enterprise wiki, which is a traditional wiki optimized for the enterprise environment and that serves as a collaboration platform system. (**Note:** a wiki is a collaborative Web site that can be changed by any user who is granted the right to edit a given page or section. A popular example is Wikipedia.) Enterprise wikis are used to run a project development space, a document management system, a knowledge base, or any other groupware tool on an Intranet or on the Internet. Today, TWiki is being used for everything from project management and knowledge management to CRM and support databases.

5. Product: Multiple.

- Link: **www.project-management-software.org**

- Their Claim: Web-based software can surprisingly increase performance, productivity, and efficiency within an organization. Since Web-based applications can be accessed through any Web browser, no desktop installation or updates are required. Web-based applications require being installed on a server, which is most of the time hosted by the software developer. Moreover, certain providers even offer Intranet solutions, which can be installed on your own server.

  Our directory lists developers who offer effective, 100 percent Web-based business tools. Their applications are accessible by users from any computer, at any time, from anywhere. Programs available include:

  ° CPM. Web-based project management software that shares multiple projects, tasks, and calendars.

  ° Autotask. IT business management software for Service Providers and Value Added Resellers (communications companies).

  ° Ace Project. Web-based program for multiple users or projects.

  ° Parature. Web-based customer support deflects up to 80 percent of incoming service inquiries.

  ° Vertabase. Project management software providing full service training and support.

  ° Interneer. Application platform providing flexible project management software, allowing users to track, control, and manage data. Features include dashboards, Gantt charts, reports, and workflows.

○   Team Manager. Project management and collaborative software providing Gantt charts and showing dependencies, groups and rollups, resources, calendar, and more.

○   Bug Track. Web-based issue tracking system allows for unlimited users, projects and bugs, and customer support for a low, flat rate.

○   CRM Desk. Automates online customer support and knowledge base via the Internet. Designed for companies wanting to provide Web-based support for their clientele.

○   XPD Office. Project management software providing features such as data entry, collection, approval, reporting, and mail. Integrates with MS Project and accounting packages.

About the Author

Elle Bereaux spent 20 years in the telecommunications industry, where she rose from an entry-level clerk to a director. She now spends her days managing real estate investing firms and writing both fictional and educational works.

Index

A

Activity 18, 39, 49, 64, 71, 85, 86, 89,
92, 98, 99, 102-108, 111, 113,
114, 116-123, 126, 128, 129, 133,
135-139, 148, 149, 155, 163, 164,
168, 170, 172, 178, 183, 185,
191, 192, 195, 196, 204, 215,
217, 219, 234, 245, 255
Approval 47, 50, 60, 61, 64, 77, 78,
108, 199, 207, 213
Assignment 64, 67, 75, 110, 228, 234

B

Build 25, 34, 59, 78, 80, 82, 88, 113,
123, 126, 137, 140, 176, 183,
190, 201, 207, 211, 215, 253, 261

C

Communication 17, 18, 51, 52, 72, 93,
143-147, 164, 170-172, 179,
204, 216, 218, 223, 225, 228,
233, 236, 242, 253, 256, 263
Constraints 51, 61, 74, 77, 86, 92, 93,
101, 112, 113, 124, 127, 135,
155, 170, 180
Content 59, 101, 181, 238
Costs 48, 62-64, 69, 71, 76, 77, 85, 86,
92, 93, 99, 101, 102, 130-133,
135-139, 146, 151, 152, 169, 170,
178-181, 183, 185, 186, 194, 211,
212, 224, 235, 236, 244
Criteria 74, 89, 92, 142, 175, 245

D

Deliverable 57, 61, 67, 71, 74, 80, 82,
89, 92, 97-99, 107, 110, 127-
129, 139-142, 145, 148, 150,
153, 155, 156, 168, 174, 176-
180, 182, 189-193, 197, 205,
207, 208, 210, 212, 213, 216,
242, 246, 252, 259, 262

E

Execute 18, 63, 87, 97, 168, 189, 193,
223, 225, 245
Exercise 25, 43, 71, 79, 89, 102, 103,
117, 127, 132, 135, 139, 173,
192, 197, 249

F

Focus 17, 30, 33, 34, 48, 75, 136, 155,
179, 182, 215, 224, 232, 252, 256

G

Goal 27, 35, 39, 40, 42, 43, 54, 69, 70,
73, 83, 126, 128, 153, 158, 162,
245, 246, 252, 263, 264

M

Management 17, 18, 21-23, 28, 29, 34-
37, 39-44, 47, 50-52, 54, 55, 57,
59, 60, 62, 72, 73, 77, 78, 86, 90,
93, 94, 99, 112-114, 118, 125,
131, 135, 138, 140-142, 145,
150, 152, 155, 156, 170, 172,

175, 182, 184, 185, 187, 204,
210, 213, 215, 219, 221, 223-
234, 236, 241-245, 247, 249-
252, 254, 255, 256, 260, 262
Member 25, 27, 30, 35, 55, 76, 82,
83, 97, 104, 109, 112, 125, 142,
143, 148, 149, 159, 168, 195,
196, 206, 220, 221, 243
Money 78, 101, 132, 136, 140, 178, 211

N

Network 64, 85, 103, 104, 105, 111,
114, 124, 129, 165, 243, 262

P

Phase 41, 60-65, 71, 73, 76, 78, 82,
83, 85, 87, 88, 135, 152, 155,
156, 167, 178-180, 182, 183,
187, 189, 191, 193, 194
Plan 18, 47-49, 54, 61, 62, 64, 65, 74,
80, 86, 92-94, 97, 106, 125,
135, 137-139, 142, 144, 146,
147, 149-153, 156, 159, 165,
168, 170, 172, 174, 181, 182,
189, 191, 192, 207, 211, 213,
227, 245, 251, 253, 256, 261
Project 17, 18, 21-23, 28, 29, 33, 34,
39-45, 47-55, 57, 59-65, 67,
69-83, 85-89, 91-110, 112-123,
125, 128, 130, 131, 133, 135-
153, 155-157, 163-187, 189-
199, 201, 203-221, 223-236,
241-247, 249-257, 259-263

Q

Quality 23, 40, 43, 47, 70, 74, 80, 86,
89, 92, 97, 98, 101, 127, 128,
130, 135, 140-142, 151-153,
167-169, 178-180, 182, 191, 245

S

Schedule 42, 43, 47, 49, 54, 64, 74, 76,
85, 89, 91, 92, 94, 97, 98, 105,
106, 108, 112-115, 117-120, 123-
126, 128, 129, 141-143, 146, 151,

152, 163, 164, 166-171, 173, 174,
176, 178-180, 182, 184-186, 192,
194, 201, 203-205, 209, 210, 217,
220, 221, 227, 236, 250, 252,
253, 260
Skills 22, 26, 34, 37, 39, 48, 51, 52,
54, 57, 69, 72, 79, 81, 164, 167,
170, 172, 175, 179, 187, 195,
204, 216, 243-246, 249, 257
Sponsor 18, 21, 43, 49, 55, 60, 62-65,
70-76, 80, 87, 89, 91, 92, 95,
97, 114, 125, 140-142, 144-146,
152, 153, 156, 158, 164, 169,
171, 174, 175, 178-182, 189,
191, 193, 194, 197-199, 201,
203, 205-214, 216, 242, 246,
249, 253, 255
Structure 85, 88,-90, 149, 217, 227
Style 17, 35-38, 55, 63, 168, 213, 224

T

Team 18, 25-28, 30, 32-35, 37, 39, 40,
42-44, 48-55, 63, 67-69, 75-83,
90-94, 96, 97, 99-103, 106-110,
112, 114, 124-127, 130, 131, 135,
139, 140, 142-144, 146-149, 151-
153, 155-159, 161-168, 170-175,
177-182, 185, 187, 189, 191-196,
198, 203, 206, 210-214, 216,
219-221, 225, 236-238, 242, 245,
246, 250- 256, 260-263

W

Work 17, 21, 23, 25-27, 30, 34, 35, 37,
38, 42, 43, 48, 51, 53-55, 59, 60,
62-64, 69, 74, 76, 78, 80, 82, 83,
89, 91, 92-95, 97-100, 102, 104,
106-108, 112-114, 123-125, 127,
131, 135, 139, 141, 149-151, 156,
160, 163, 165, 167, 168, 173,
174, 176-179, 181, 184-186, 188,
192, 195, 197, 203, 205, 207,
209-211, 214-216, 224-226, 229,
231, 234, 236, 237, 246, 247,
249, 250, 254, 261, 263